Essential Things

Essential Things

An Anthology of
New South African Poetry

Edited by
Andries Walter Oliphant

Published by COSAW
(Congress of South African Writers)
PO Box 421007, Fordsburg 2033
Johannesburg, South Africa

First impression 1992

Typesetting and layout by Shereen Usdin
Cover design and motifs by Andrew Lord
Cover art by Kay Hassan

Repro by Repro Print, Johannesburg
Printed by Galvin & Sales, Cape Town
(8291)

ISBN 1 874879 08 7

Contents

Introduction

This anthology of twenty-three poets developed from, and is released into a literary and cultural context made up of numerous traditions, differing concerns and divergent tastes. At the present fragile moment of transition it is a terrain fraught with conflicting meanings, interpretations and evaluations.

Forays into the field of local poetry have been marred by simplifying and distorting tendencies governed by crude and rigidly monolithic views of what poetry should be. South African literature has consequently been bequeathed with a legacy of clashing exchanges which produced little insight and failed to cultivate a sense of appreciation for the existing body of work. Where a sense of the multivalence inherent to poetry and an appreciation for the multiple localities of the South African context are called for, the history of poetic reception is regrettably replete with one-sidedness, parochialism and aggressive aspirations to dominate.

The framework of this conflict assumes a dualistic form. On one side, the articulation of private, personal and subjective themes are complacently equated with excellence by those inclined to a conservative outlook. According to this view, any exploration of historical and social themes is inevitably accompanied by aesthetic impoverishment. This perspective is problematic in at least two significant instances. Firstly, a dangerously stunting and prescriptive aesthetic philosophy lurks in this point of view. Secondly, the fallacy which postulates a necessary correlation between poetic themes and quality confuses taste with evaluation and fosters an intolerant, biased and fundamentally uncritical attitude.

On the other side, and equally debilitating, have been calls by radical poets and critics for social and political relevance at the expense of formal and technical accomplishment. While this sterile debate froze all meaningful discussion, poetry itself was never entirely trapped within these two mutually reinforcing forms of blindness. Accomplished poetry, self-evidently, depends on the extent to which form and content are synthesized or deliberately juxtaposed to constitute an intelligible and significant articulation. Thus, far from having to start afresh, it is to this basic understanding of poetry as a significant form with infinite formal and thematic possibilities that poets and critics must return. Now that the old social molds as well as the crude oppositional and defensive patterns of thinking are dissolving, this perspective will, hopefully, emerge more clearly.

The compilation of this anthology was guided by such a perspective and is 'new' in at least two senses. Firstly, and rather pedantically, it is the first publication of this body of work. While some of the poetry appeared in journals, and a handful of individual poems in compilations, the bulk of the poetry has not appeared in print before. The main aim of the anthology is to introduce poets who have as yet not published full collections. In the case of exceptions where poets, like Ari Sitas, have already published individual collections, the motivation is to include a selection of new and previously unpublished work. The anthology includes a substantial selection of work which reflects the main themes and styles of each poet. It is consequently made up of a number of individual collections.

The second, and more problematic sense in which this anthology is 'new', resides in the stress placed on new themes and forms of poetry. In a modern context which links creativity to the production of new ideas and commodities, innovation and novelty have become central aesthetic norms in literary and cultural evaluation. However, I am aware of how, in the words of E.E. Cummings, literature like love is a realm in which 'anything old' is very often the basis for 'everything new'. It is therefore important to keep in mind that innovations are carried out in relation to a context or a tradition. The American poet Mark Strand, writing in *The New York Times Book Review* of 15 September 1991, expresses this double process as follows:

> It is a difficult task: to speak through the poetic
> and linguistic conventions of a particular time
> about that which seems not to have changed. Each poem
> must, to a certain extent, speak for itself, for its
> own newness, show its ties to the conventions of the
> moment and its distortion of them. It must make us
> believe that it belongs to our time even though what
> it tells us is really old.

What is presented as new in this publication is a selection of work which stands in relation to the entire text of existing and emerging forms of local poetry. In my view, the innovative impulse is registered in the movement towards dissolving rigid boundaries between subjective and idealist poetics on the one hand, and public and materialist aesthetics, on the other. This aesthetic dissolution is marked on a formal level by the openness of poets to different styles and the willingness to combine diverse modes of expression. The newness of this is not so much the claim of radical innovation but the consistent emphasis this direction receives in this publication.

The procedures outlined above yielded a variety of voices with divergent and frequently overlapping concerns. By drawing on poets from different parts of the country as well as from the work of poets who have been in exile until recently, a range of different localities and sets of preoccupations found their way into this collection. It resulted in a anthology of great variety which takes its title from 'The Condemned Men' by Mxolisi Nyezwa:

A new way of expression
saying the same essential thing
in a new way....

A concern with the tension between basic and persistent facts, problems and demands of human life in a constantly changing world which drives poets to search for and invent new ways to express what is discerned beneath the surface of appearances is disseminated throughout this anthology. If the title's 'essential' has a metaphysical ring to it, it is counteracted by the plurality of 'things' thus marking the contradictory movement which informs poetic labour in the process of giving form and meaning to experience.

The anthology fully displays the stylistic heterogeneity of the poets in the range of lyrical, narrative, dramatic and performance poems it presents. In evidence too, and particularly refreshing, are the syncretic forms and languages wrought from oral and popular musical traditions. The tones projected by the individual poets are equally wide-ranging and the anthology asserts this multiplicity. In an era where the desire for reduction and a simplified, predictable aesthetic order relentlessly impinges on creative writing, the poets published here affirm the multiplicity and connotative plenitude of the poetic utterance as it speaks of human experiences, the world and itself.

In conclusion I wish to thank Frank Meintjies and Baleka Kgositsile, both members of the COSAW Editorial Collective, for assisting me by reading and evaluating manuscripts for this project.

Andries Walter Oliphant
Johannesburg 1992

Mxolisi M. Nyezwa

To Have No Art

here

here we only have knowledge
of the one
that spewed
the one heart that gave in

here we only have the future
of the embittered soul
the clattering cart
and the dying horse

here we cage-in men's larynx
gravitating the vowels
that key language and communication

here technology and all its implications
is a skin's pigmentation
black fumes the charcoals
that spill cold blood on man's brain

reluctance

the night is the night
final
the day is the day
final

I am neither of the two
it's that simple

final

attraction

it is the feeling, the element
within
not the power,
it is not capital, not the sacrilege
of seeing men marched....
it is none of these things.

it is something legal
not by the laws of the land,
it is the vortex of the muscle
within
it is not the rush, the hope
of seeing beans sprout....
it is none of these things.

it is not the stone that lies
straightened-out
smooth and slippery,
it is not the green algae
that covers its sharp edges —
it is something deep within
that moves within its blood.

it is not the hurricane, the hail
the cold sleet
and the delirious rain,
it is not the hardened storm —
it is not something that emanates
from Heaven's side....
it is something from the other side
of Paradise.

it is not the ordinary people
that are to blame,
we don't blame
for setting this earth in motion....
it is the recess, the subconscious living —
the things that moved Freud
and man's anarchy.

it is the co-existence
it is living together, the warm//(final)
symbiosis...
and the space in which we circle
draws its radius back

silence

they don't say it
they don't say that once there were people, a
village of huts, strong men and log-fire,
they don't say that people used to build there
with reed, thatched roofs and stone
they don't say it now there was a river
that the children used to go to
they don't say that people used to give sacrifice
there

jokes and dreams

i haven't come here
to mourn the ruin of a dream
i haven't come here
to shed any tears
i haven't come to restore
what was supposed to be the final
masquerade
i've come to witness how hard
the wind blows
beneath the dark forest

i haven't come to shake hands
with neat demons in golden attire
no! not from these shall
i choose my friends
i haven't come to see the withering
of a yellow bud that rests
against a passing wind
i've come to be a part of
another dream

wind innocence

it's a blue blue wind
that blows
god's people away
a crazy crazy day
that mocks
the poverty
paling god's people a trifle more

barracks

my mum says
too much of anything brings a man emptiness
too much thought
clogs the mind
too much fury
fails the heart

so too much of anything is an inner emptiness
too much love
pains the heart
too much sadness
wearies the bones

and inside the vacuums of our lives
the universe is a turntable
spinning endlessly

the children are gone

no longer strange
no longer
like the earth
like the human spirit
it's not strange
not unfamiliar
we've left those feelings
many rains ago

they are dead within us
transformed
into the human void
that re-chains our empty clarity
that sculptures each man's fate
and breast-feeds our poverty
we've left them...
abandoned

it's not new
we tell them — that is
should they ask
have the strength to inquire:
'where's Thokozile, where's Dumizulu?'
and we look at them
with only cold tears in our eyes

poems and papers

but not for now
you sat, you looked thwarted
knowing what the moment meant
(at last hell has constricted
your soul too!)
you laugh, you dance no more
my good friend

things change
at least then, it won't be like this
it will be a totally new suffering
like when a baby sucks
his thumb

it will be a totally new experience
(for God and history has provided)
we won't have to blow our minds
about it

it will be like a fresh song
from a sparkling songbird
it will be like that for us, as an old
woman sits neglected

on the chair of her memories
it will be fresher, more vital
for us...at least it won't be like
death

and like the death we die
every moment of our lives
it will be a totally new suffering
it will be like a song sung free
from a careless heart

(our failure will have its dignity).

Old Guy

you could be thinking
this is not for all, not for the boys
playing in the soil's earthiness
not for the child, the virgin girl
nor for the women (cold and crooked)
this could remain thus, feeling alone

the dustiness of the street pulling
your boots, you could be
thinking, lying on the wet grass
seeing the swallows pass
a kite in a misty sky

you could wish, feeling so odd
trapped in a drifting dream
feeling the earth and its keepers
the birds in the trees, heavy in heart
and still this woody plan
all this bizzare and dying kingdom

you could moan and groan inside
poor like a slave, knowing of the heart
knowing of the greasy dismay
the shoddiness of the day
and an all rehearsed episode

and I hear your brief sigh
I sense your anxiety, following
a forgotten path interspersed with stones
our minds filled with archaic words;
and you could stare and stare
across this age,
you could rest a happy man

Hiking

it is not the first time,
you read out a poem to me —
antholes
in market streets
with men with gaping skulls
watching the universe

the world conveys meanings
in strange ways,
we swing, feet straddled in the frozen river —
reaching out for high-life and meaning

with teeth full, *Selected Works
of Wally Serote* —
we jump from city to city,
laying blame on ignominious men
with cutting briars

The Condemned Men

and almost all hours
in the stillness...
between the uneasiness
of dawn and night in the consternation
another day
(another dismal day)
almost...
we repeat it to ourselves
as we recall

regret
as we rely on instinct
on change and untrustable destiny
weighing all on history and a dream
'what we wish the turn of events'

as we stagger we mutter it
to ourselves
thinking only of survival
here where borrowed means forge man's
ultimate action
where the road never ends
muttering
how cold nights twinned us here
like rats caught in icy lakes
sensing defeat, and thinking — really
is this it
how it all clicks together
the final point of our journeying

searching for it
(after all those nights, those
cold nights)
the hope never dies
it must never die
it should never die
our hope has to find other means
of survival

a new way of expression
saying the same essential thing
in a new way
in a different medium

as we curse the stars
we curse the heavens
the life around us the life beneath us
the dead life beneath us
bent and crooked
as we're scurried across

perpetuated
like dead pictures — unbelievable
like still-life
flown across our existence
bent and crooked

and yeah again we sense it
the strangeness of wasted life
coming strong
(not enough not good at all)
how men's policies reshape our past
the years of our search
the days of our peril

now our lives are invisible
our being here immaterial.

To Have No Art

I hate the sunshine
I hate its
twelve hours
that fly like the swallow
and the sea-gull
fly
leaving a dead melody
in my throat.

Baleka Kgositsile

After the Rains

Where is Home

Tell me
where is home
Is it the hotel room
which hosts
this grand occasion
which presides
over this honour
which delivers to me
the first sleep
inside my country
after 5148 nights
away from home
down the thin road
of personal history
roaming
in search of home

Tell me
where is home
Is it the cluster
of mud structures
which surround
my father's ageing body
and lonely heart
is it the thorny path
to the family graveyard
could it be the shade
of the tall trees
whispering above
my mother's grave
or the sacred space

which permanently holds
her body away
from my hungry eye

Is home the house
in Lusaka or
my children in it
Is it the flat
I sneak in and out of
unnoticed
where is it
Is it the elusive roof
turning me fast into
an olympic candidate
as apartheid grins
at me daily
its green teeth
mocking my enquiries
systematically turning
my coming home
to a jump
into a bottomless pit

Listen
is it the corner
on Leopold Street
packed with women
children and belongings
night after winter
night while fate
sits huddled
in a warm corner

watching...
biding its time
eyes glued
on the boxing ring
to our surprise
left to words
thin-legged words
without gloves
flying round the ring
not even a referee in sight
is this it

Where is home
tell me
Is it childhood
memories that weathered
exile storms
is it the square
shoulder that supports
my wet face
where is it
I search the eyes
of my comrades
while we toyi-toyi
on the back
of the truck
which is breaking all
speed limits
heading irreversibly
for Mhlanga rocks
where...where is it

What shall I tell
my children's children
Their birth was postponed
when history possessed by
an unspeakable zeal
poured thirty years
of golden honey
into the dough
of the home cake
where is it
please answer me
is it in the kneading
basin or the oven
where is it
my womb asks persistently
while faithfully clutching
at the bouquet
of feather dreams

If home is South Africa
a country on the
continent of Africa
if it is the world
sprawling across planet earth
let it have
a plate of food for all
let it fill
winter mornings with
the sunshine of human
goodwill pouring from hearts
of clothed women
men and children

free from homelessness
free from fear
free from jealousy
free from humiliation

Let it come
with torrents of rain
to wash away
bloodstains tears and gall
of yesterday
let this moment
turn into home
the bull's eye of the
prisoner's focus
as minute after ticking
minute defines and moulds
dedication and discipline

Home
the heart of hope
for the scrawny youngster
'I don't know where home is
violence or forced removals
moved my village'
he says and continues
to arm hundreds
with the art
of fighting a disciplined war
his love of home
an elaborate song
known best by his heart
and the sands of Angola

Let home feed music
into the silence
surrounding the memory
of the ex-prisoner
let home be
an unfolding dawn
ushering in the new day
where my daughter
will be seen and
judged as a person
let it bring us eyes
that will see
voices that will sing
the beautiful things
around us
let it be
the symphony that
will massage
the tension lines
from the weary heart
of our people
that will water
the seed of a future
determined to be born
that the children
of this country
be midwife and parent
to HOME

Voices

As long as
our voices look
into each others
sad eyes as
long as they
touch as
long as our
voices hold hands
as long as
they embrace
as they float
in the tense
silence of the corpse
littered night
WE WILL LIVE

Pietersburg

I leave you
behind heart trembling
table top land
stretching across time
beyond my short memory
Blouwberg mountains
wait over this shrine
where my birth
was hatched
watchdog mountains
wait over this shrine
where my childhood
steps were contemplated
and cautiously taken
table top land
you held the wrist
of my heart
in the midnight
of desert years
my feet traversed Botswana
the eye of my memory
the ear of my heart
made contact
with the echo
of your landscape
Mimosa land
flat like my spirits
as I remember
the last visit
before the drought

guided by the best
of your daughters
who lies in waiting
for the great celebration
when the harvest
will be on
continue to cradle
the fountain of love
and hope
that oozes from
the soft face of my grandmother
Nipple of my childhood
I leave you behind
YOU ARE IN ME

Flames On Ice

Who are you
what are you
the voice rolls
the words like
drums of sea water
raring to be calmed

Don't they say
only the gods
know these things
when father declared
'the one who sets fire'
did he know
of the flames

that would leap
on solid ice
forty years
down the road

Who are you
I ask of the
two deep wells
above your nose
where dark waters
murmur and dance
in the nordic night
Yes
restless ghosts
have followed from Africa
now we loom
over this operation table
we must perform a caesar

What are you
the question lingers
in the chilly morning
like a heart turned
snow white thousands of
mountains away from home

Son of woman
did you see the
slow trickle tracing
a thin path down
this dry cheek
This is pain

braving a look
into the face
of a prodigal
twin brother
This could be
the end of the search
for a long lost sister
open your eye

See deep
deeper than the bottom
of the Scandinavian lake
that ripples and hums
throws its shining lace
in the air
as it leaps glides and
tumbles with the green
land leaving my eye
uncertain if it
has been witness
to a love game or
a battle over space

See the red
of the rose
echo of the rhythm
of the heart
yearning for a song
See the wound
where my breast
used to be

Listen
know the sound
of a dirge
is this the
voice of a spirit
singing a requiem
for all that could
have been that
never will be

Are these the
strains of a serenade
defying the boundaries of
a viking grave
rising with the
golden orange that peeps
from behind distant hills
on a mission
to celebrate life
In other words
is Sergel Plaza
a labour ward?

Akwaba

Mystic child
where do you come
from where
are you going
teeth lighting up
weary hearts around you
though your own
remains wrapped
in cobwebs

Akwaba
a spectre approaching
arms ready to envelope
those who shiver
in the noon
of a summer day
But suddenly
you turn into
the vapour that
rises from the Indian Ocean

You are the song
that stops the dazed
from being the dead
but where...
where are the voices
with which to
join the singing

Akwaba
the whisper
that rides the wind
from diamond land
that flies through
the 'free' state
which screams
for freedom
that rolls on
to the platteland
for decades in
the throes of labour
sweating...wishing
for a competent midwife

You are the knowing
unravelled silent
face of Mona Lisa
did I have a peep
into your soul
I know you
want to be touched
you yearn for
a long piercing look
into your eyes
where diamonds lie
lazily wishing
to be mined

Akwaba
guitars horns and
drums wailing and
rolling converging from

the four poles
wishing to hold hands
in an anthem
for humankind
begging for an arranger
'stop the war'
Where is the maestro
to mould the notes
into a fist of
harmony raised like
a flag of peace
high in the
morning air

One Of These Days

the sun will rise on us

At that point
where our names merge
like siamese twins
it is there
we shall find the truth
beaming at us
like this moon
that hangs above
our womb
this car

Yes
let the sun rise
on this heart

that struggles to pump
while coiled in 'shame'
let it rise
and reveal that
the green of the grass
does not come from
words spoken in skyscrapers
far from the soil

The sun should rise
and melt particles
of shimmering silver
that froze the smiles
we used to know
it should open wide
the doors of the human
heart and mind

Let love walk
with the calm confidence
of a girl
who knows the art
of balancing a pot of
water on her head
let her feet know
this landscape intimately
let the echo
of her voice
bounce like a ball
from hill to hill

Let the sun rise on us

Teach Me the Song

Mothers
of my forefathers
on a morning like this
when my heart is bursting
with the rays of the sun
filtering through
the humming leaves and branches
when I am overflowing
with the crisp song
that rolls
with the golden leaves
and I want to be
an echo
what do I do
when I want to sing
to the world
and my tongue shrivels
into a dark corner
of my head
and the lips in my head
say
I do not even know
the name of this tree
or the bird
that sang me
out of yesternightmares
what song can I sing
tell me
you who composed
songs that retrieved mankind

from the jaws
of huge monsters
whose skeletons
today pose safely
in museums
tell me
teach me
the tune and lyric
that will spray my heart
into the air
before the particles rain down
on the earth into
a loveprint

Lindelwa

You've heard only a cold silence
from me since that night
that quiet summer night in Matola
which turned suddenly
into a grimace
into a shriek
whose voice was the blood that
sprayed walls and floors
soaked beds and clothes
clung to skinbits and bones
sipped into soil
to quench the unquenchable
an Indian Ocean night
that turned into a desert

If I were to summon back
daily Thyume River crossings
from our joyful days
if I say come
in the morning let's cleanse
our eyes with sungold
that flickers like lovethrobs
in dewdrops perched like teenage girls
on grassblades
I could say
come in the afternoon
let's watch tree leaves
poised like birdwings waving
lightlaces from the retreating sun
or come in the evening
let's seal bonds
in plates of maize and beans
or in the quiet night
let's hear Thyume waters roll
in bubbles of music
let's float on her
and rummage her green bottom
will it end the winter
in our soul

If it melts the icicles
around words that emerge
like dust from the ruins
let's do it
let's do it
so we can grow like a tower
of tough legs and hands

and ears and brains
all rising into a monument
of our children's future

Ma

I pushed your letter away
I blocked its stab
for a moment
now I sink slowly
in the crimson river
that gushes from your words
for hours I drown
in the drums of blood
that pound on your nights
I squirm amidst sparks
that explode in the temples
of your days

There are lessons to share
we must survive
In pursuit of freedom
we roam jungles
where our flesh and bones
get crushed between
the teeth of wild beasts
Yet we survive
even when the jungles
we roam
are the heads of madmen
we survive

From Ipuseng

Mama
my children calling
calling me away
from the anaemic and dazed
bottom of despair
they keep calling
Mama
I hear voices calling
calling from ancestral authority
urging me to give birth
Mama
they call strength
strength into every vein and artery
strength to give birth
Yes to give birth
to my people

Guess Who Did It

Last night after you sang to me
after you'd danced into me last night
we watched moonlight games
on the sleeping land
with shadows of spying trees
melting into the connivance
we soaked in the quiet darkness
and let the hand of calm
ferret dust-covered pockets of strength
tucked away
in corners in us

Today I took a walk
around the block
it felt like a holiday
in a far off land
I know I can be the green
of the shrivelling plant
with double eyes I see
confidence in the banana tree
flapping its elephant ears
the birds' song is sweeter
Today the rainbow flakes
of children's voices
caress the morning air

What Do You Say
From Willie

What do you say
when you have
these wings that propel you
to heights and depths
which defy measurement

But this here
this now
is not free
from unhappiness
this here and now
is a shiny blister
of turmoil

Between these punches
that are our life
when you drift to the edge
where the sea meets the land
ride on the waves
and let life reclaim you
moving deeper and deeper
ransacking this maze
for every bit of life

When Will the Sun Shine

I
There goes my heart
with the winter sun
to sink
in the horizon of hope

II
It's midnight
the announcer says
it's midnight
the end of songs
that crashed into my head
scattering thoughts out
it's midnight
I grope for a memory
that will give me a light
it's midnight
next to me
looms a void
that follows me everywhere
that firmly plants itself

wherever I sit or lie
it's midnight

III
I am tired
of the company of thoughts
that lead me
into a cold tunnel of longing
the backbone of my patience
longs for the long arms of sleep
tomorrow
the sun will shine
into my soul

Come Back Boykie

Yesterday
your eyes retreated steadily
from the sockets
further and further away
far into your skull,
last night
your buttocks stiffened
the rectum was pulling
intestines coiling slowly
into a compact snake
in your hollow inside,
today
little snakes bulged
in your temples
they wriggled and spat
poison into your temples,

tonight
your snores have been chasing rest
between grimaces and half-blinks
up and down ragged hills
in and out of ravines
the night has been shuddering
with rumbles that jerk
your contorted body
in depths that quake
with the growling
of these monsters you encounter

Listen
the night air carries other echoes
listen and be soothed
hear healing whispers from Oodi
home of crocodiles
that gave you a ride
into the night of the unknown
listen to a vigil song
that sways with the slapping waters
remember
remember those depths that glow
with the moonlight as they
gurgle their eternal song
over a thousand pebbles
companions of the mother spirit
that keeps vigil
in defiance of years
though her body was swallowed
by a grave we must find
her spirit hovers in the moonbeams

that breathe on crocodile backs
Come back Boykie

Here is a kind and firm hand
from the proud land of Yemen
the hand of Yemen has delivered
a twin mother spirit to us
ties of love have been tightened
with the umbilical cord
come back
take the hand of the queen
who must be led to Oodi
to the mother spirit
Be here tomorrow morning
when history scrubs her mouth
and the monsters dissolve
down the drain
with the bitter sour slime
that will be flushed out
even from the throat
Come back Boykie
Come back

4 Mwembeni, University of Dar es Salaam

I
From your windows we watch
the beautiful mothers of Africa
we see them come and go
everyday
their backs groaning
under the weight of
New York London Bonn...
their black faces
flashing defiant smiles
their big hearts pumping love

II
At the height
of Dar es Salaam's humidity and heat
we were wrapped up
in a dry winter of nostalgia
you were an island of comfort
massaging our heart and soul
to move
away from malaric inertia
towards Sasolburg

III
It is true
you are full of sores
that fester
yet it is from your windows
we've made acquaintances
from the trees around you

we get a shade
When our nights have been drenched
in a fever of unfulfilled desires
and restless memories
the green and gold leaves outside
wave in the Indian Ocean breeze
to calm us
the morning sunlight
seeping through the wire gauze
melts the frozen marrow of our hope
melts the frozen blood
in the veins of our minds

Blue train
taking us through months
with day and night
joy and pain
issuing through your pores
cocoon of reassurance
we keep afloat

IV
There's a magnet there
often when I'm lying here
it sucks me out
I wander around
scratching and picking
with the chickens
when the clouds frown we croak
and cower away
when the first drops fall
after the rain I bask

in the smile of the sun
and sing with the birds
free
I crawl with the lizard
and creep with the snake
In the afternoon breeze
I mingle in a hum and dance
with the leaves and branches
with the grassblades
sometimes the night inhales me
I float about the sleeping houses
fused with the whispering darkness
spellbound
till the morning stealthily joins
in the quiet ceremony
There's magic all around
green gold red orange
it is there
with the tree trunks
so firmly rooted in the land

After the Rains

And now after the rains
the land smiles

After the rains
a woman smiles

The sweat runs off her body
when it rains
so she smiles

But the cancer that gnaws
at woman and land
runs deep in the veins

Let's Get Together
To a monitor lizard

Child of nature
stranger to my ghetto experience
you drew more than a foot long
of desire to know you
while my eye was glued
to where you slowly
disappeared into the grass

Only now that I am here
Here where our illusions
drown in brown bottles
and gongo sips
Here where the poison
of two-legged reptiles
threatens to be deadlier
than that of a mamba
Here now I make your acquaintance
child of nature

how could I know you back there
in the beloved forest
where rectangular pockets of misery
mushroomed to the rhythm
of greedy vultures

How could we meet
when you had been
whisked away by monopoly
and all that remained
for me to perceive of you
were grotesque shadows
suckling fear and suspicion
How could I?

Yet even now
some will laugh at my 'strange'
preoccupation with you
as if you were not there
when nature gave birth
to us all
as if they do not feel
the pores of the continent
itching with the lice
that are 'leading'
its children to doom
as if I should be ashamed
of extending my hand
to you whose viciousness
I do not know
(although I hear your tail can be rough)
to say let's get together
child of nature
we move on the same land
let's get together

The Hill On 8. 7. 81

This morning
loneliness is closing in on me
the last of our countrymen left

we know though
of those whose fangs
dripping with the blood
of our children
stick out behind
european passports
we know their stench

This morning
the claws of loneliness
stretch out
towards my throat

Party
For Jamela, Bruce & Jim

We carve
this moment
deep in the wall
of our times
we dance
all weakness
and aches away
we move all curtains
and let soul

touch soul
we dance
deep into the past
to reclaim the drum
whose song
binds us
we dance
far into the future
when we will have
built a monument
of love and peace
and dance

Shut Your Mouth

If you struggle with me
I might appreciate it
If in the process
some of your blood flows
I'd even embrace you
If at some point
you start a word game
and mention 'sacrifice'
I'll know the past
still stands between us
and I'll spit you out
HARD!

Exile Blues

let them roll
let the blues roll out
but 'this load is heavy it requires men'
has nothing to do with baritone or beard
it is a word of warning wisdom
when the uncountable miles
between you and home
the beautiful land
you vowed to liberate
become unbearable
and you ask yourself
if it is worth your leaving loved ones
as if you left home
a victim of a stupor
when having been rejected
like vomit
you try to examine
if it is the food that is stale
or the stomach that is sick
when you are threatened by paralysis
in the midst of so much to be done
when pettiness has played so many games with you
that like an addict
you cannot remember when you did not crave
just another piece of gossip
when the demon trinity
inferiority complex
self assertion
sadism
have so become your masters

that you put the stamp
on your own death certificate
as you try to destroy a comrade
when you drink yourself insensible
into the gaping dark void
that is ready to receive you
like the vicious jaws of a shark
when comrades have fallen victim
to mental breakdown
and you shudder wondering
if you won't be the next to be ambushed
when you make a habit of exchanging blows
that should be kept for the enemy
when you feel trapped
suffocating
at a cul-de-sac
and your tears roll down uncontrollably
as memories invade you daily
maybe let them roll
let them roll down the blues
let the blues roll out
till oblivion sneaks to your rescue
when later you feel lighter
retrieve the zeal that made you leave home
lest you go down the drain
with the stinking rot of history
when the song goes
'this load is heavy it requires men'
that has nothing to do with baritone or beard
it is a word of wisdom and warning
that our history is so reddened
with the best blood of our land

the enemy gets more vicious by the second
because the enemy knows
'victory is certain!'
is no empty slogan

Baby Boy

You and I
have made a connection
through wire
and space
you and I
have made a connection
through the dance
of yesterday
and the song of today
whose clear note
glimmers and rolls
down the valley
of a thousand hills
I wish I could say
'Karibu'
But bloodriver
floods the land of Shaka
I wish
I wish I could have
arranged a grand
reception for you
yet the air chokes
in the smoke
of the baby boy
who never saw
the sun rise
outside the womb

Mark Espin

Territories of Doubt

I believe that the world is beautiful, and that poetry,
like bread, should be for everyone.
— Roque Dalton

Memoir of an Elderly Woman

All I want to do now
is to live the rest of my days
savouring the wonderful hours
that arise so unexpectantly;
at being able to breath
and feel life manipulate
my faint heart.

I have had a good life.
Today I can recall
the times when I helped my mother
at the large, white house
where she did the laundry.
I still remember sitting upon
an upside-down cast iron bucket
watching her kneeling on a cloth
at the side of the bath,
hunched over its porcelain edge;
her hands deftly working
the thick piece of blue-green soap,
twisting the wet clothes,
wringing them dry and then again
rinsing the mass of material
until it was suitably clean.

When all the washing
had been done and after
we had arranged it
upon the long washing-line
in the back garden,
we would always wait
at the kitchen door
for the lady of the house
to come and place the pittance
in my mother's grateful, outstretched hands.

There are many times
when I begin to wonder
what became of that lady?
She always seemed so aggravated
in that large, white house.

Afternoon in the Shade

> *It is our knowledge that dismembers us*
> *and puts us together again with those things we denied.*
> — Yannis Ritsos

The whitewashed pots of geraniums
enhance the stone-paved stoep.
The wine evaporates from the bottle
provoking the neurons of conversation.
The gnarled trunk of a glorious oak
rises into the infinite entity of pale blue.
The frenetic pace of transport
across a nearby bridge
fails to sequester the unity
of our languid theorising.

The mild afternoon relapses,
and the time we occupied
shifts into another sphere,
compels us toward discoveries
that our minds have yet to encompass.

Third Eye in the Gloom

On the outskirts of the metropolis
the churned up earth is dumped.
Wheels turn against the day
lift ore from great depths.
Down below men sweat profusely,
break stone for bread and sleep;
headlamps the third eye in the gloom.

Gumboots squelch in the puddles.
The cocopans roll along the rails
pushed by men with wet
bandannas on their heads.
Outwardly the miners endure
abuse from racist gangers.
In the dark caverns
the stench of rotting wood
overwhelms the ritual of work.

The Highveld night is cold.
Winds wail through disused structures.
Activity at pithead increases
as the shaft elevator ascends.
The headlamps are doused for another session of sleep.
In the middle of the mine
danger patiently awaits human error.
Corporate executives are nonchalant
like vicious gods about a sacrifice.

Attempting a Poise of Thought

> *Every emancipation is a restoration of*
> *the human world....*
> — Karl Marx

The road passed through an unending
flatland of low shrub and sand dune.
A breeze was moving inland
over the sea and the lagoon.

Inside the cottage
he made a fire
in the coal-stove.
His body felt fatigued
but his mind was filled with energy.
As the fire expanded
he watched the gesturing flames
through the opened hatch
until he finally fell asleep
in the warm stillness.

The breeze of last night
was now a gale, shifting
the sand of the wide beach.
He considered the wreck entrenched
at the north-eastern end of the lagoon,
and walked in the opposite direction.

After rounding the protruding sand bar
he discovered a multitude of yachts
moored at the landing point.
The sight of the billowing
sails delighted his heart.

He returned to the cottage
and arranged a place of comfort
on the small, wooden porch.
The view across the water
Stirred his creative urge.
He gathered a pencil and paper.

The lines and tangents that appeared
on the page, fused into a vivid composition
of the natural completeness of the water
and the gulls and the horizon.
He completed the sketch, turned
his head to notice a neglected cigarette
smouldering in the ashtray,
burnt out to its filter.
He leaned back in the comfort of the chair.

The water of the lagoon was luxurious
He lazed in the water and the sun
weightless. The low waves rushed
over his body. He felt
his head lighten, closing his eyes,
feeling the mass of liquid against his flesh.
A ream of evocations from the past
moved through his mind.

Still the conflicting currents
moved his body in the yielding water
changing its position all the while.
The water became the universe.
The forceful currents
became the constant challenges
within his mind, the tensions,
the tides originating
from disparate directions,
closing in against his body
sweeping him along
His body retained
its form and its balance
in the struggle of
water against water.
His thoughts exert their particular energies
upon each other, keeping the mind intact
like the activity of matter that suspends
the earth in perfect levitation.

He emerged from the water
slowly, self-assured, less perturbed
about the water still surrounding his legs.

Tragic Year

I
This has been a year of tragedy;
grief penetrates the heart.
The maelstrom of anger spirals
onto the tongues of the wounded.
Hatred for the enemy corrodes
the lives of the young.
The deranged potentates
deliver their speeches,
and the country oscillates
on its axis of pain.

The frenzied pace of time
lapses into the mundane.
Troops in battle fatigues
patrol strategic points;
search for the clandestine
trafficking of guns and grenades.
Bland reports disembody
an inflamed sense of loss.
During quiet moments we mourn
the deaths and incarcerations;
remain determined to resist
the demented dogma of obese men.

II
The various patterns of partial light
are dulled by the slow blaze of the sun
as it begins to cross the day.

Remnants of a gale shimmer
twists the stem of a daisy.

A single bird chirps ignorantly
perhaps satirically;
sent by them to fool
and to entice.

It took flight and shrunk
to a speck of reconnaissance.

There are no human sounds this morning.

The placid atmosphere insinuates
a tremor, that may yet disturb
the flat monotony of everything.

The untrusting bird returns
with armoured men in steel trucks.

But violence fails to exorcise,
only exacerbates the strife.

Lines Written in Depression

I
As I sit on the edge of the ocean,
my eyes chase the ends of rainbows
and as if in an epic irony,
a wreck is taunted
by the malignant caress of the surf.
An immediate urge overwhelms me;
to wade into the gargling belly of the sea,
and enfold into the labyrinth of a shell.
The vivid becomes surreal.
Suppressed notions keep mushrooming
and finally exposed, bubble uncontrollably
like confused or awkward thought.

II
The day tucks in behind the clouds.
The moon wanes, like a reposeful spirit
and the gleam of a lamp rises.
Thoughts are sketched in sullen forms
on a discoloured ceiling.
Dusk's distorted images coalesce.
Shimmering mosaics of light on water
form a workshopped son et lumière.
Mild and languorous
a wind flirts
amongst darkening dunes.
Now cold and alone
I listen attentively
to the heaving of trees
and the moribund rain.

III
Spring rain falls vertically
bending the blades of grass;
revitalising the parched sand.
Birds warble continuously.
Rivulets of air channel
a mild freshness.
The mellifluous breeze soothes,
inspires a spore of vitality.
Stream of water falls;
ripples through the weary head.
Liquid noises fill voids,
imbibe into my heart
save it from exile of aloneness.

Langebaan 1985

An Argument

A cult
is manufactured.

We stand
and watch
the pyrotechnic
display of words
enthrall
the captivated
as it invades
the neutral
spaces of thought
annexing

the territories
of doubt.

Minds formed
within the throes
of brutality
seem to imitate
the harshness.

Self-portrait on Campus

Heads muddled with syllables
traverse the passages and the halls.

I stand in the shadow;
observe the confused dance.

My heart whirls
around the trees.

I see my face in a pond
and a goldfish passes
through the liquid of my eyes.

I am like the water lily
that exists nervously
on the surface.

Observations on a Visit

1. Brixton Road, Brixton.

A train heaves across the bridge
above the street where vehicles
are negotiating their journeys.

I simultaneously forge my way
through the throng of people
who trample the sidewalk.

I look across the road.
On the island in the middle
of the road's juncture,
I notice a young woman
seemingly meditating on the lawn.
Her hair has been coloured crimson
and into her nostril she has inserted
a gold or silver ringlet.

Quite slowly she draws
out a cigarette and a metallic lighter
that glistens in the morning sun.
She squeezes, the head of the lighter
which sets out an orange flame
that rises higher and higher
until her face and crimson hair
disappear behind it.

II. King's Road, Chelsea.

The sultriness of evening emerges
in the view across the square,
dominated by an elm tree
and blue park benches.

Red double-decker buses
ride up the street
that has been activated
by the procession of people
from market to market.

The symbols of glamour
are paraded within the galleries
of the affluent, who pose
in the accepted fashion of the present.

Outside post-modernist restaurants
post-modernist motorcars
decorate the gutters.

III. Kentish Town Road, Camden.

I am near a narrow canal.
Its waters are almost still;
move imperceptibly through the sluices
and deviances constructed
in times of primary industry.

Amidst the rush of noise
and the panic of desires,
lovers embrace, secure themselves
from the intrusions of those concerned
only with the vertigo pace.

This image of placidness;
of stillness between two people
is rapidly overwhelmed by the intensity
and frenzy of existence.

IV. Hyde Park

I walk near a flat lake.
The moisture sweeps against my face.
Beneath a Victorian bandstand
an orchestra produces sounds
that flow through the thrush
and vanish over the grassy rise.

London 1990

Surrealism in Bellville

In the crisp light of a Bellville morning
the day stretches over the whole sky
and hangs from the edges of the half-moon.
The horizon swallows the spring clouds
that form a duvet of darkness
upon the streets and car-parks
where bits of rubbish
perform a ballet in the wind.
Buses, trains and taxis trek
like seasonal migrant birds,
bringing people to buildings
constructed in robust architecture.

Work has become a habit;
like smoking, or picking
your nose. Batteries fail,
lose their acidity. Our
nervous systems go down,
cannot be connected
to a specified host.
We wait patiently
for official announcements.
They always make good reading.

Fragile

Night. I am sitting here
listening to a Yaqui
Indian folk song
played by Keith Jarrett.

The sounds of the piano
drop slowly, is measured
to the heaviness in my heart.

I cannot stop replaying it.
Its romantic aura
has engraved it
upon my mind.

Nothing happens
apart from the loneliness
inside the silences
of this song
that tumbles
through me
like a wave of sadness.

Morning. The melody
winds down through
the placid darkness;
stirs the dawn
to its rendezvous
with light.

The indentations
of ink on paper
reveal blotches of thought
that wisp away
like thistle-down
lifted from its stalks
by a light gust.

The morning envelopes
my static senses.

A blade cuts my lip
and blood slips
like a dewdrop
from a leaf.

I see you in the sun now
and like a rainbow,
your body seems as fragile
as the fragments of light.

A Rumour of Dreams

The clichés of violence
still infiltrate, still permeate
the utterances of our speech.
The allegories of death
are still prevalent
in the images of our thought.
The orthodoxies of the patriarchs
still dominate our lives.
Yet, within the midst of this brutality,
humanity has eclipsed the degradation,
and from the vistas of our minds
dreams have unfolded, have evolved
like petals from a calyx.
We have begun to assert ourselves;
to mobilise our consciousness,
to banish the strictures of ignorance
and the hideous mythologies of fear.
Together we must sculpt and pare
the forms of our various lives
and in all ways possible
celebrate and urge our thoughts
to move in this cycle
of ever renewing cycles of life
and to finally create
a vibrant aesthetic of our being
so that we may hold
our lives in our hearts.

Mzikayise Mahola

The Other World

The Other World

The deep running water is
A fortress filled with
Lores and mysteries of Xhosa
Its depths hide answers
To numerous questions
Its powers hypnotise and transform
Others succumb to the calling
And join the people from the other world

I'll Remember Yesterday

Tomorrow I'll hoist our flag
Blow the anthem from my horn
Like a village cock
Under its shade
Rest myself
And with disrespect
Remember yesterday

Under the flag
I'll smother my sorrows
Breathe a sigh
And share my experience with the young ones
They must know
Life is a priceless gift

We can forgive these evil deeds
But what winds can dry
The fountains
Of our memory

The Weight of My Soul

To Keorapetse Kgositsile

There's music in my ears
Loud, soft, distant and clear
To purge myself
I want to sing
To purse my face
Defiles my breath
So I curse

In a song I want to put the weight
Of my soul
When I marvel at nature's wonders
But where's the weight
If I only curse?
I'm afraid
I'm afraid to hurt
Kgositsile the great
So I use this rotten tongue
As an excuse
To shut my mouth

Kgositsile you're a bluesman
Sing me the lyrics
Of your ballads
And teach me how to sing
To release this soul
Like a bird up in the sky
Let me fly
And never pine

How Could He Understand

At another place
We would have been friends
No mistrust fear or hatred
Pushing us apart
Not proud fools
Fumbling in the dark
But clean and apartheid free
Like drunk orphans at a feast

He didn't understand
My friend didn't
Because our love was cold
So he quipped queer questions
Victim of a strange world
'I understand how it is for you
To be black
And I would like to help
But there's nothing I can do.'
Under the dark skin
Fumed the human in me

How could he understand
That I also hurt
When he was so blind

So he went on
And asked it
'Don't you sometimes wish that you were white
When you can't get what you want?'
I was appalled
Astounded and horrified
He wouldn't understand
Why the path of a troubled man
Zigzags like a trail
Of a wounded beast

The Hogsback Mountains

The steep mountains of Katberg
Locked with the Hogsback
With the Winterberg
Form Lushington basin
Awfully high to strangers
And equally high to travellers
Look climbers on the head
Yet too shy in rainy months
Always hiding in the fog
On wintry days
Sleeping under snow
A haven for a thousand hogs
Wealth of the mountain tribe
Flora and petra
Pride of nature's finger
Carved for the tiny souls
A freedom from mankind

I long for their berries
Wild fruit and game
Miss cliffs and waterfalls
Spewing fury in white rage
That petrified me as a child
Mysteries of nature
Springs and streams
No drought could tame
Their water is nostalgic
I yearn for stock and crops
Produce of the peasants
The generous soil
A pleasure to the tiller

I miss the vulture's plea
Keen to caress a carcass
Of a horse that has served its master
But everywhere I went queer looks followed
Names of childhood friends
Had never been heard
Where their homes stood
Now tall trees grow
And where I was born
A big dam smiles
It has swallowed the past
I wanted to scream
Of course they'd whisper
I told you! He's mad
For answers I look at the mountains
With tiny footprints
They were frightfully huge
Could those baboons and game

Which we used to hunt
Recognise me for old time's sake?
I felt thirsty but springs were dry
Willows, oaks and stones
Had they lost their special names?
I stayed away from you
Place of our spirits
But your pulling force
Binds me like a spell

The Snake in Human Hands
To Nimrod Mkalipi

It took us unawares
Yourself unprepared
This bizarre exit
Though enmity was declared
Between man and the serpent
Coiled like a chain of lies
You took the snake in human hands
And it confirmed the scripts

I plead silence from all
Let him pass in peace
Roll his knapsack
And wash our hands
The snake fulfilled the curse
Roads will bear his prints forever
To where the journey ends

We need no priests to mend our hearts
Opened by scalpels of physicians
Searching for the sting of death
His young ones want him home
To steer their ship of destiny
Through turbulent seas
Humans have to cross
Death confounds scientists
They haven't found the planet of the dead
Noah sent a dove to check its wrath
For he didn't know the den
Jesus met it on the cross
And witches stole the corpse
With the bandit they wouldn't swop

We'll send no priests
Their minds are in heaven
Scientists will build research stations
Politicians have forked tongues
And poets twist the truth
We write unfinished stories
Each about his mission
And after we're gone
The world talks of our deeds

A Hen Crowed

A hen crowed at the door
Inside a woman panicked
Throwing her child onto her back
She sped cutting the zigzagging path
Her breasts hopping to match
Her alternating buttocks
as she fled into a grove

A man chopping wood
Saw a hill of human flesh
Advancing towards him
He gave a sigh 'Mh!'
'Nomhi! what happened to my child?
How is your hut?'
'Mola Tata, I am very well,'
She panted sweating
'Then what chases you my girl?'
'Tata, I'm here for I'm scared
A hen crowed at the door
And I was alone.'
'Mh...Mh!'

They went back home
The man relighting his dead pipe
A howl broke the numbing silence
Again he let out a deep sigh
Stood up and went out
Embarrassed and troubled he chased the howling dog
'I haven't heard from my husband Tata,
Maybe he's found work
And can't find time to write.'

Her father-in-law spoke looking down
Avoiding her stare
As if blaming the earth for his problems.
His wife had been dead for eight months
'Father! the hen and now the dog!'
Her voice faded into a whisper
'Nomhi, I'm thirsty.'
He accepted a tin of water
Which he gobbled thirstily
She sighted people coming down the grove
And shook hands with her father-in-law
They discussed weather, stock and family life:
Then there was silence.

The Omen

The owl perched on the roof
Cursed like an empty grave
In the hut
People could not sleep
The dog kept howling
They whispered like mourners
In a house of death
Shaken
In the long night

When the woman woke her husband
He played dead
The fire was gone
In uncompromising darkness
Who sent the owl?
They must find out
Bakuthath 'unontongwana

In the morning a tree dassie dawdled in
Like in a drunken stupor
There was pandemonium in the hut
All cursing and swearing
Till someone clobbered the rascal

They went to see a Sangoma
Who asked a heavy fee
To open his sack
Baboon and monkey bones
Rattled the feared answer:
'I see death in the family
An evil woman is chasing you
It is a close relative
But I can return the spell to her
For that my payment is a cow.'
'Mhlekazi sinyuka nengalo.'
'Of course your house must first be secured
She will retaliate
That goes for a thousand rand
It is a big job.'
'Proceed Mhlekazi! Proceed!'
'But you will pay the spirits first.'

Carrying heavy hearts
Full of saddened news
The horses returned sauntering
A little boy came out
To meet the sullen souls
But carelessly came too close
The horse
Frustrated by the boring journey
Vented its wrath with both hooves
And his name was taboo

I Cannot Talk

Whispers, whispers and whispers
Whispers in the air
It's even in the trees
Branches in silence whisper
And I use my stinking breath
As an excuse to zip my mouth
Because I cannot talk

When I walk in the street
Silent eyes gnaw my flesh
And I gallop in madness
When the wind blows through my bones
The world gaping through windows

Listen to the wind
Do you hear something?
Is it lamenting my silence?
P-a-a-r-r-o-o-ts! You stupid birds!
Caged and trained as dummies

Were you made without brains
But with a voice so loud
To shout me down?
Listen to the ghosts
Their tongueless skulls whisper
In the night through the mouth
As you sleep
P-a-a-r-r-o-ots! You ugly birds of prison
If I could talk
And train a peacock
To laugh you dead in your cages
Or set a billion bees upon your beaks
I'd peacefully suffer in silence

Prayer

Soften the warlords
With human kindness
Fill them with grains of conscience
Suckle the running impis
With milk of love
and put the serpent to sleep.

Hell's Doors

A lonely wail of grief
From a gaol of solitude
Like an abandoned cat
In a deserted house
If you stop and listen
Words fall like snowflakes
On hard white rocks
The painful cry has a message
I'm the abandoned child
Envying the birds up in the sky
For though they may cry
They can fly and
Sing for all to hear
My heart does not beat
Stuffed with words I cannot say
Where is the joy of life
Serenity singers sing of
Everywhere all the time?

I cannot sing the pain in my heart
And so I shut my mouth
Though it defiles my breath
Then I cry to give it vent
In quest for peace
But peace does not come in the mind
When alone in bed
I can't sleep
Tormented by songs
No one wants to hear
People say I'm crazy
Fit for institutions

But what prison doors can silence this heart?
What grey walls will muffle cries
Hollering like a dejected orphan
Condemned with a bitter soul
Without direction?
Like a problem child
I'll shout all the way to hell's doors

The Calling

Nomvo stooped by her father's side
A bedding with a bundle of bones
Listening to the whistling sips
From tortured lips.
Where is the origin of this norm?
Old people want a morning cup in bed
She mused
Then remembered her dream:
'Tata! I dreamt again last night.'
'I'm listening, my girl.'
'I was collecting wood in the forest
With other girls.
I came upon old men
Sitting in a circle
Dressed like diviners
With white clay.'
'M-m-m-h.' He forgot his coffee.
'They asked me to join them
I tried to run away
But a dog checked me
And I obliged.'
'M-m-m-h.'

'They asked for my name:
Clan name and ancestoral names.
I recalled some
Then they shook my hand
Saying the search had been long.
To welcome me they slaughtered an ox.'
'I'm listening.'
'It ends there
I was woken by barking dogs.
What does it mean, Tata?'
'Can I have another cup of tea please?'
The subject was dropped.

The silence of the night
Was broken by a sharp scream
'M-a-a-m-a! T-a-a-t-a!
Yho-o-o yho-o!'
'Heyi! Nomva wake up!
What's wrong?'
'I had a bad dream.'
'Tell us about it my child.'
'Shut up woman, leave the child alone!
Go out Nomvo
And talk to your ancestors
We'll hear the dream tomorrow.'

In the morning
Nomvo related her dream:
'You have sent me to my uncle
And I got lost in the forest.
I came to a river,
On the other side were people
All in white, beckoning me.

I entered the river
And I thought I was drowning.'
'M-m-m!'
'Iy'emntwini Mbhele!
Itheni le ndoda?'
'Shut up woman!
Who is the man here?
Have you forgotten my stick?'
'I'm worried because these dreams mean something.'
'Don't tell me what to do
I'm the bull here
And that is final.'
'He who scorns advice
Reaps tears.'
'Did you hear me, ma Radebe?'

A few days later
Mbhele saw a party of men
Lazily coming over a koppie towards him.
'Molo mfondini!
We were told we'd find you here,
How are you?'
'My family is healthy
My stock is well
But can I hear about you?'
'We are in good health.
We have something to discuss
It is delicate.
You are white people
Your child has been called
Now her safety rests on you
Because nobody must cry.
You must find a way to inform your wife

You know women
They are strong and weak.'
He was stunned
It had long been coming
It was in the family.

I Can't Write Poetry

When I read songs
Of greats like Soyinka
Okigbo and Serote
Elated I fumble for my tools
Intent to thank their lives
For sharing them with me
Foolishness stifles my aims
I get muzzled

I need no one to tell me what to say
Only how to say
In skills I'm limited
Mother is my sweet witness
She sent me to school to improve
Seeing I was such a fool
So when I'm quiet
I cannot speak
For my mouth is full
Full of gratitude
For the help of others

I'm Sorry You've Missed Your Flight

It's a sea of faces
Expressing indifference
I'm desolate
Emotionally
Numb and oblivious
From apprehension
Fate gives no indication
Of what lies ahead
I came, saw and stumbled

I'm sitting staring
But unseeing
Minutes and hours pass
Like fortune
Will they pile up to days of doubts?
I'm a particle
Of insignificance
In this multitude of aliens
They come and go
Leaving me to my misery
That life may continue

How could I have forgotten
That these are but pains of growth?
How could I have allowed myself
To be the prisoner of fear?

Twenty two hours have passed
I'm still waiting
Life is continuing
Can't undo its plan
Except to note it down

How Will I Trust

I was born an automatic
Guided by signs
All my life conditioned
Now I'm adjusting
On my own
Measuring each step
Like a chameleon
How will I trust my ears?

I've been hurt
Physically and mentally
Seen things
Not fit for mortal eyes
My children saw me kicked
Like dirt thrown everywhere
But I bear no grudge
Only struggling to adjust
How will I trust their tongues?

For an ice breaker
I went to sea for a swim
Nobody cared
Even the water was not stained
By this river squid
I was surprised
For I've been called names
How will I trust my eyes?

I am not impotent
Nor are my offspring barren
That I should forget the past
Destroy historical records
As I savour dawn
Testing the ground
Like a newborn calf
The leopard might strike
How will I trust their word?

To Frizbee the Dolphin

When the deep sea exiled
Leaving you to die
At the Van Staden's Mouth
You had no choice nor chance
But to submit to fate
In silence face the unknown
Warm and loving arms
Embraced and caressed your soul
And gave you name and home
To start afresh
Shy at first but you soon settled
Uncomplaining in your new life

Your charming antics
And princely elegance
Mesmerised the world
From far and wide crowds came
Swept by this love
With the force of a wave
Prince of the seas
Till death broke your life
Leaving much to be said

Blood Turned Acid

For my brother

Behind the mask of pain
With a smile of grief
Lies a tender heart
With blood turned to acid
Wrinkling your soul
At the death of your wife

I question my mind
Oh feet of mine
Carry me away from this scene
Where death made its mess

Though one womb conceived us
Of different spirits we're made
Round and around you
Your brothers and sisters join hands
Clapping dancing and singing
To see you mend and rise

With a smile on your face
Rise sweet brother, rise.
Brave brother to the finishing point

Rest in Peace Dear Brother

Oh! Thank you brother for your life
Your thirty-five years with us
was real sweet
From mother and father
We were nine
Now we are stunned

One by one we take off
Scatter by choice and force
As we learn to fly
Into the waiting world
To be strengthened or destroyed

You took an early soar
And the storm was too strong
Sweet dreams a mirage
We were not on your side
When you made the deadly plunge

The long search has ended
There's nothing left but pains
For melancholy waited
Wrapped in white calico
Cold as death
In the mortuary

You left us scattered in the world
Yet so close to you
We could hear your sobs
But not hold the soul
There's nothing left

The Law of Attraction

I wonder what they dream
When they plant seeds of hatred
In tiny heads
I wonder where they'll be
When it's harvest time
I wonder if the silent world
Will remember
The role of its indifference
When a thousand Strydoms and Delports
Are unleashed

There Was No One

No one could tell us who came first
Gugu
Or the Hogsback mountains
He toiled hard to the summit
At first with willing hands
A hermit of ages

In silence he fed travellers
Broken by the mountain
With water from a spring
Oiled many a dry throat
Avoiding any human stare
Till age plugged his ears
Fogged both eyes
And winters locked the joints
Of his rusted frame
Forcing him to crawl like a crab
There was no one

There was no one
When snow banished him indoors
There was no one
To feed the dogs
When he froze to death
The snow thinned and vanished
The stench took over
The dogs became restless
Unable to overcome the pangs
There was no-one
When they forced their way in
Except those rocks
To witness it all

Never Ever

It has been hard gaa!
An endless nightmare
Let's make sure it never recurs

Swallows Are Arriving

We were born in winter
Deformed by blistering tempests
When storms veered southwards
Most were caught on their backsides
Many were swept away by this force
Others doddering like aged
Somnambulists in the dark
Happily and expectantly

Those aware of prophesies
Rang bells rejoicing
Hollering to wake all:
'Amandla ngwethu!
Mayibuye i-Afrika!'
At the breaking of summer
To see the sun,
To flex, to stretch and reconstruct
The blind adjusting to light
After decades of darkness

The Colour of Love

I queued at the bank
Between white ladies
A ham in a white sandwich
With a toddler pulling at my pants
I grinned tempted to scoop her up
This tiny angel appealing for love
This conditioned robot
And smiling dummy
Feeling crowded
I remembered Grahamstown
Where a black boy went too far
And was taken to court
For kissing a child
The law served him right
He might go far too far

The child was insisting
I was resisting
To take her in my arms
For the mother was restless
Glaring at me warningly
She snatched her to safety
Wise mother
Who knows
I might go too far
But the child started yelling
The adult stares almost killed me
Yes I understood
But refused to move
For I can be mean
when a child is denied

Mavis Smallberg

Signals

A Small Boy

For Gilly Nyatele, aged twelve, written in response to an
article by Sarah Sussens in the Weekend Argus *of*
25 August, 1986

First the face, and then
the caption caught my eye:
            Small Boy Seen As
            Threat to State Security

The face is oval
the cheekbones high
the mouth a generous curve
and then,
those eyes!
The eyes are almond-shaped
with wrinkles underneath;
those eyes show largely white;
the expression in those
serious sullen eyes
is a danger to the State!

A small boy should not have
such eyes;
eyes which glower, two black coals
smouldering on the page;
eyes which cannot seem to smile;
eyes unfathomable
filled with hate, or tinged
with fear?

eyes which look as if they've
never known a tear
a small boy should not have
such eyes

A small boy should not be
detained.
A small boy should not be
in jail.
Not once,
not thrice,
not four times in a row!
A small boy should not be
shut into a cell
so that he can break
a small boy should not be
a danger to the State!

And yet
that small boy knows the slogans
knows he has to fight
a system which pays his mother
sixty rands per month.
The small boy
fights against grown men who
pose as 'vigilantes'.
The small boy
frowns when comrades drink
getting drunk inside shebeens.
The small boy
with a hundred others who call
themselves 'the fourteens'

'run the place' — Tumehole,
a township in Free State.
This small boy
just released from
Heilbron prison in Parys

But right now
the small boy only wants
'to eat and eat and eat'
he fidgets in his chair and says:
'white children sit in chairs
like these'.
The small boy talks about
democracy
and says his brushes with the
state has only made him 'stubborn'.
This small boy,
this Gilly Nyathele,
who with his three brothers
live on salt and porridge
and who, together with his sister,
often hungry goes to sleep.
This small boy knows his fate
and wants his country
free

Ah, woe betide our fate
that such
a small boy
is a danger to the State!

Abattoir Road

The stench of woollen urine
and manure waft in
through my window.
Bodies tight ahead
stacked.
A nose, with neck
strained upward
or snatching at the air.
They stand
stand
stand in thirties
forties
fifties in the hot
still summer air.

An encumbering wooden plank
cuts up an ear
slashes an eye
a dumb animal eye.
A silent signal
of a dry, dry
mouth gasping
black dense smoke
that the monster
expells into the air
as it slaughters up
the miles from there
to there.

'Livestock vehicles right'
I pause behind
as the monster grinds its teeth
snorts at traffic lights red.
Red like the blood
that's soon to flow.
Red like the stain
of the dead trodden dead.
Red like the danger
their quivering nostrils sense.
Red like the meat
served on my plate.

Happy Birthday
For Anton Fransch

It is the generation of Bonteheuwel '85
Ashley   Colene   Robbie
now Anton

'organise and mobilise
shh! shh-shh!
get out your AK
kill a man —'

A man died last night
in sedate, quiet Crawford
a man running and jumping

against the wall
over the wall
up a wall
down a wall
he was behind THIS wall

but here is no wall

Oh, a mean man-made machine
came lumbering, plundering
maneuvering down a sedate, quiet Crawford street and —
wham-bam! thank-you ma'm
fluttered down the wall

on the other side of another wall
it is Melanie's birthday:
Happy birthday to you
Happy birthday to you
Happy birthday —

look at what the police have put on display, Melanie
they're inside our house
showing their guns and rifles
and handcuffs and keys
and barking monosyllabic instructions
without saying please
and Melanie's mother cannot
bake a cake.
If I knew you were coming, I'd've —
hired a grenade

Look Melanie — fireworks
blue lights
orange lights
red lights
bright white light
bang-bang! rat-a-tat-a-tat-a-tat-a-tat! bang-bang!
There is so much noise, Mummy!
Why is there so much noise?

Look at the intricate spray
of little holes in the wall
very neat, very round
a lethal bouquet
and here's a mangled door-frame!
Look at the strip of splintered spikes
showing white inside the dark stained frame.
There are holes in the wall
the size of a man's head
bleeding red dust.
There's a huddle of feathers....

Afterwards she climbed through the shattered window
the mother of his child.
When the owners of the house fixed the fence
against those who had come to gawk
funny how the chickens didn't squawk.
She stood and watched and looked
and walked around
stooped to pick up freshly fired
charred bits of paper
and stared at a train time-table
pasted on the wall.

Did you see the dead white chicken
in the yard
bloodbright against the white?
Funny how the chickens didn't squawk.
His mother said his stomach was out
his head was okay
his face was okay
but his stomach was out

'organise and mobilise'
'shh! shh-shh
get out your AK
kill a man —'

You're ten years old today, Melanie
and the generations of Bonteheuwel '85
Ashley   Colene   Robby
and now Anton
wish you a very happy birthday

For James Matthews
After reading Nadine Gordimer's The Black Interpreters

So James Matthews is not a poet.
     what
     is a poet?
'A writer in verse' — James, the un-poet,
     perversely not versing
     and thus not deserving the title of poet — or
     what?
     is a poem
'A metrical composition especially of elevated character'

Ha!
there is no pulse
there is no beat
there is no rhyme
or reason in
James Matthews wrote the following:
                    'democracy
                    has been turned
                    into a whore
                    her body ravished
                    by those who pervert her
                    in the bordello
                    bandied from crotch to hand
                    with her breasts smeared
                    with their seed....'

Indeed!
indeed   indeed   indeed

Why is it that those lines
pull —
why is it that those
            beatless
            rhymeless
            words strung together
            hither thither
            helter-skelter
tug
            at the place within me
            makes that place contract
            and then relax with the
            gentle shuddering of a
            breath held

and then released in
tiny soft just-audible
gasps

Yes!

yes   yes   yes   yes

Perhaps, James, your poems do not have an

'elevated character'

but then
does that matter, and
what
does that make me —

a poetaster?

Funny Thing About Words or Sorry, I'm Not Allowed To Say That

Words, in themselves, are not false;
People are.
They treat words too lightly,
bandy them too easily.
Their words become meaningless,
carry no weight;
are particles of dust, destined always, to settle
for just the briefest of whiles,
before they dissipate.

One cannot blame words.

What else do we have, but words?
They shade our every meaning
can be clinical, cold, exact.

They twirl, whirl with our happy feeling
stoop with our stumbling,
run away with our longing,
can be down-to-earth
or matter-of-fact.

What wonderful, magical words are:
peace   justice   love   friendship
democracy.
On the other hand, you have
corruption   evil   detention —
socialism?
Now there's a magical word for you!
Some people block out words like that.
Want them wiped out, covered up,
not even whispered —
c-o-m-m-u-n-i-s-m?
In places you can get killed for saying a word like that.

Be careful with words.

People with big mouths and usually big sticks
don't like hearing certain words.
They'll stick pins through your tongue
so they don't have to listen
to any such words.
Not even a magnificent word like
sharing.

You can go to prison for saying
some words.
Like...sorry, I'm not allowed to say that.
They ban reams of words in newspapers, on radio,
television, in books, magazines, plays,
poetry.
You are only allowed to gesticulate wildly,
or preferably, just nod.

The big sticks would love a
perfectly silent world
Just a nod-nod here,
and a nod-nod there.
Then they could own all the words,
or utter only those that they choose.

But that's the funny thing about words.
They cannot be owned.
Like weeds, they insist on coming out,
even if only scribbled upon walls
And the nodders,
those who have grown comfortable
in their gesticulating world of silence,
sometimes surprise even themselves
when suddenly they whisper:
Amandla!

The Frog

I wake to faint soft shuffling
of insistent feet.
Drowsily I peer over the bed's edge:
There, a dainty little frog
brown speckled,
with beady pinhead eyes
blackbright
sits in frog position
on the floor

So frog
you too like moth and man,
hanker after light.
And now, with tiny silly leaps
you try to reach the globe
just above the floor

What am I to do?
I cannot sleep with you so
close about my head.
What if with one supreme athletic leap
you land upon my face?
What if you should light upon my sheet
And I awake to find
the shiny up-side-down frog shape
imprinted on my cheek?

I know:
The cat!

I open up the door;
she comes sniff-sniffing in.
Oh! she knows about your presence, then
I move the bed
to lighten, ease her task.
Sorry, Frog.
You hop,
I leap upon the bed.
I cannot bear to see you crushed,
I do not really want you dead.
But I cannot
have you in my bed!

With swishing tail
she taps and waits.
You do not move
you're playing dead!
She yawns and settles down to wait.
That's just not fair!
It's nearly four
and still you sit froglike
upon my floor!

I read a book.
My feline friend is dozing off,
and whisper soft you move away —
I know what I will do:
I'll take a bucket with which I'll cover you
Tomorrow, when my braver friends awake,
they'll set you free
and I will smile and tell them
how you pestered me.

I stand
poised with bucket
in my hand....
You hop
I leap —
My feet!

You disappear behind an empty shoe.
Dear Frog,
I've had enough and so have you.
You're miles now from my bed.
The cat's asleep upon her paw.
I'll shut the light
and in the darkness that ensues,
we both will sleep and
darkly dream
how light might mark
our freedom in
the morning.

For Barbara and Gail

School Staffroom
during
School Boycott

clickety-click   Black humour
one purl   Black Oppression
one plain   Black Confrontation
s   the small ball
h   of   w
a   h
d   i
e   t
s   e
of Madame Defarge   s
teargas outside   curl up
the staffroom   purl up
purls   knuckles white
l   tension gone
u   a
r   s
i   t
d   r
jokes   a
New Japanese Contraceptive: y
HOYOKUKITOU   long strands

Have you heard?   of yarn
Pik's changed   w
his surname to   e
SWART   a
b   v
l   e
a   clash
c   Black
k   White
                      Red
                      Pink

    clickety-click
    one purl
    one pain

Signal

I received your feeling in the post
the other day
whittled
to a single, solitary
[!] mark

This signal
bold, mechanical
unleashed a whoosh of animated feeling
titillation, delight

that you, too
liked
the other night

Supermarket Encounter

I move on my two
good, strong legs
in fact
today my feet are
thrust into shoes with
heels almost eight centimetres high

agony poised on my brow
I tripple disgruntled along
my feet make me aware
that deliberate discomfort is wrong
and there's no need
to concede to fashion

you whoosh by
your hands deftly spinning
the wheel
your two weak, useless legs
stick out in front
and there's an eager
bright look in your eye

my pain lames me
shames me

For Our Mothers
Everywhere: especially in Valhalla Park, Guguletu, Athlone,
Bongweni, New Brighton, Mitchell's Plain

Black old ladies have the most beautiful smiles
their face's glow
gleam
like deep purple

Purple: royal, mourning.
Black old ladies compare
They mourn the lost loves
the lost lives
of sons and daughters maimed
killed
and three-year-old grandchildren
shot
at point blank range

Yet lack old ladies still smile.
They dream of a long black tunnel
ever widening
enveloping the white
squeezing it
obliterating it

Black old ladies make magic
in black tunnels.
They make pig faces shrivel
make odd-shaped grey and blue overalls
which billow out into the strange shape
of even stranger men

spin endlessly
till their shapes disappear
into a pulpy soggy blur

Black old ladies are magic
in white-seeking black tunnels.
They discolour grey and blue overalls
uniforms
twist them
and hang them out to dry

Royal
purple-clad
Black old ladies mourn.
But next time
blue Overalls
you see a Black old lady
stop
and watch her smile

On Reading *Sturdy Black Bridges*
Edited by Roseann P Bell, Bettye Parker and
Beverley Sue Sheftall

I wonder what they'll say about me
when I'm dead —
        She chronicled times
        without literary merit?

I wonder what they'll say about me
when I'm dead —
       Her words are too simple
       Her language is clear
       But her work lacks good metaphor?

I wonder if they'll know about me
when I'm dead —

Will they find all this paper
slipped into plastic and stacked
quite neatly with dates at the bottom?
Will they just take it and throw it away
these scraps of my life
these bits of my heart
will they just chew it
and tear it apart?

I wonder if they'll bother about me
when I'm dead —

I don't really care what they'll say
when I'm dead
I'll be dead —
deader then dead
But I hope
I so hope
That some tiny line
will stick in her head

James Twala

Family Planning

Family Planning

Row upon row
like winter-shaken stalks of maize,
the barracks stretch from one
miserable end to the other.

Within the enforced hostel
no gay children bounce and romp about,
no busy housewives colour
the washing line once a week.
Here there is no homely smell of food
that wanders in the air during the day.

Sunset gathers the half-castrated inmates
like stale crumbs from the city.
They plod through the large gates
weary, bent and shut
their fatigued minds, eyes and ears.
For them the day is over.
They are banished to a twilight life.

The silence that they left behind
at the breaking of the dawn is
rippled as if it was a calm lake
by laughter as they buzz about
like newly-wedded women.

They strip off to their vests
embalmed in a day's sweat.
Yesterday's tripe and porridge are
hastily warmed up for supper again.

One by one,
they enjoy their naked showers
splashing their rigid bodies in the water,
and return to their stuffy rooms.

An inmate belches like a sea-rover.
It echoes in the far-flung room.
He raps his full stomach
that is large as a mole-hill:
'Exchoose me you bastards!' he thunders.

They slip into their stony beds,
clasp their baggy and sweat-reeking
pillows as if they were their
beloved ones left in the homelands.

They look at their shirts,
overalls, trousers, jackets — all ragged,
hanging aslant on the damp walls
like faded, dusty, tasteless family portraits.

Portable radios switched off,
candle flames flicker and die,
darkness and silence covers
them all like a large blanket.
Alone,
they quietly succumb to sleep.

In the night,
an inmate's untroubled sleep is interrupted.
He sits on the edge of his bed
holding his erect penis, warm and loaded with sperm

half dozing,
gazing from darkness to darkness,
and then he spills the seeds of nature
all over his slovenly sheet with half-satisfaction.
'Family Planning,' he whispers to himself.
Then the musical snores
of the sleep-drowned inmates,
slowly lull him back to sleep.

My Father

I accompanied my stocky father to work.
He carried the spade, I carried the bread and pork.
He boasted about his work, and was very pleased
about the people who were under him, who had ceased
to live a long time ago. He bowed his head
as we entered the cemetery and stroked his goatee beard,
an act of honour for the dead: The countless mounds
were adorned with flowers, eerie sounds
that are associated with grave-yards, I did not hear.
He pointed to a grave without a tombstone
and pitied the poor fellow with his hoarse tone —
'Once the chairman of Farewell Undertakers
but buried in a cheap coffin unlike the bakers
of Eatwell and Co who were toasted alive but were buried
in shiny coffins.'

He sobbed a little as we hurried to another grave.
He shrugged his broad shoulders
telling me about Mr Simpson,
a climber that met his death under boulders.

He was a bigamist too. His beautiful wives
fought for his corpse, buried by this one,
exhumed by the other.
a lot of harm was done by this disreputable family.

Some people called them witches,
some just called them silly.
With his thin smile, he read
an inscription of twins: 'John and Fred,
born on a day that never was on a calendar,
both died tragically in a car'.

He spoke sullenly about a Mr Golden,
a notorious friend of his,
tough, rough and hardened criminal
that was arrested as he was about
to pay him ten pounds.
As the police dragged him away
he promised to come back from the grave
and settle his debts,
but his six-foot grave seems too deep.

The grave next to his, was Grace's.
A lady who was supposed to be in hell.
She was a murderess.
Drunk brandy like water.
When told she would go to hell,
she smiled and said she had friends too in hell.
We walked along and reached a naked grave.
Beneath it lay the remains of a man that was a slave
to the bottle.
He died owing the shebeen a lot of money.

The shebeen owner was mean.
She desecrated the poor man's grave and sold
the tombstone to compensate.

I have seen a lot, he tells me now and again.
He pointed to a plain
grave of a bully. His funeral was a family affair.
Of course, of course,
he pointed out that it was all very fair!

Toothless

You three-rooted spectre,
terror of my mouth,
half healthy, half decayed.
I have felt your sting and insane fury
rise like dust in a whirlwind
deep in the night.

For years you stood
like a white rock in my gum,
enhancing my smiles and grins.
Now it is all over.
You lie in my palm, faceless and scarred.
You have left a hole
deeper than a grave,
dripping and clotting
and fumes of unwholesome breath
that turn my friends' faces aside.

Offal For Sale

The heavy odour of offal hangs
like a pliable branch in the air.
They are scattered like frost-burnt
leaves under a skeleton tree.
The stink stretches and sways
like smoke in the air.

The stench greets the homeward
bound commuters around.
They inhale it like
a familiar scent,
but quickly eject it with saliva
leaving the forehead wrinkled a while.

The entrails glimmer in the fading urban light.
They are teeming with large flies
whose continuous musical murmur
can be heard from afar.
They fly from offal to offal,
beating their light wings with joy.

The seller waves his bony arm over the offal.
The flies buzz off with futile anger,
but they are back again on the tripe
before his arm has swung back
He aids the sale of his offal
by crying to the public:
'The intestines are two feet longer today,
and as usual boneless, fresh from the cow!'

A house-wife stops,
looks at a digestive tract.
With a craving eye and says:
'Yesterday's intestines were bitter like gall,
I think that cow died of stomach trouble!'

A dog patiently lies on the ground
praying that the sun should set quickly.
The unsold offal will be
emptied into the gutter.
It will feast like Mr and Mrs Jones and family.

Biltong

The lean strips hang like
dead faceless serpents on the slack washing line.
The sun parches the biltong
with the patience of a housewife.
The wings of large flies
sing continuously around the dangling strips
that are streaked with dark fat.

At dusk,
a large-mouthed woman emerges
from the house and stomps to the washing line,
snaps and jerks at the biltong
as if it were bait,
then plucks the biltong like dry
washing from the line.

Inside the house
four mounds of steaming porridge are ready
and four lean-bodied children
are squatting like sleepy frogs
with their eyes fixed on the biltong.

They gnaw on the biltong
with twisted faces,
grip and tear the biltong
with their half-rotten teeth.
What is not ground well,
will be brought up
deep in the night
to be chewed a second time
like cows in the kraal.

Beergarden

The sour smell wanders lazily
from the beer-hall that is alive with drinkers.
The murmur grows louder
as more weary-footed men stream in
sniffing their battered and wrinkly shoes.
Their tattered jackets sag their shoulders.

Men with hanging bellies,
radiant and brine-cooling faces
extinguish the flame of thirst
with mouthful after mouthful of beer
and suddenly begin to wag their false tongues.

The rich foamy beer bubbles
settle and burst on their untamed
moustaches and thick upper lips.
Their wagging tongues slowly and lightly
caress the curves of their chapped lips
like lovers when kissing.

The pauper sits alone with a vacant face,
staring at the others with begging eyes.
The scale moves from mouth to mouth
like a cargo ship from port to port until it is empty.

Some men come to bury
the sorrows of the day in the
shallow graves of the mind.
But good sleep will sober them up
and the sorrows will haunt
and stalk their minds like ghosts.

Dustmen

They shoulder over-flowing dustbins
like baskets full of feathers,
spilling ashes and rubbish
as they gallop like goaded horses
after the throbbing dust-truck
like boys following a dung beetle with glee.

Their black faces are white with ash,
and itchy like a ripe sore full of pus.
They snivel their tasty and salty mucus.
Rivers of warm sweat run from
their dusty brows to be
tasted in their open mouths,
but quickly spat out
with a wobbly thick sputum
over the dew-blanketed and sparkling grass.

They shout like wild men,
roar with laughter like Vikings,
swear like old salts in a church-yard.
A soft speaking priest tries to
hold their slippery and profane tongues:
'God forbid that men speak profane words
Within these hallowed grounds, gentlemen.'
'Father, our souls are tattered
and dusty like our overalls,' they say.

Dogs tear their ragged overalls,
they lunge at their large legs
and have the last bark at the owner.

Flower Seller

The barren concrete is
bedecked with fast waning flowers.
In the beeless shady stall
she paces the concrete sidewalk
with a bunch of flowers
in her gaunt hands.

Only faint whiffs of aroma
escape from the coloured flowers
and mingle with the spreading
fumes of the afternoon traffic.

Her coarse and mournful voice is
lost amid the roaring traffic
as she cries aloud,
hard-eyed,
with a sad and sun-splashed face
that depletes her poor business:
'Flowers here, seventy-five cents a bunch!'

When the traffic subsides,
her rage unfurls like a flower:
she loses her sweetness
faster than the flowers in her hand.

Dusk

He hears the people passing by.
His hat,
empty at dawn
empty at noon
empty at dusk
is like his stomach as large as the gizzard of a sparrow.

He sits too low to be heeded
by the carefree passers-by
who stretches his neck like a flamingo.

The subway becomes quiet.
Silence surrounds him like friends.
He knows it is dusk,
a solitary dusk again.
He stretches his arm towards his hat
groping it painfully to and fro.

He staggers up and inhales the tasty smell
of home-made porridge and toasted tripe
floating in the air like a cloud,
just like yesterday...and yesterday.

Face Value

Year in and year out,
like a coin that is
losing its gilt every year,
I find myself in the melting pot.
I am minted anew.
I am turned
and tossed.
I am valued
and devalued.
My face value as a man questioned
in the odd mint in Pretoria.

The political god, illuminates my head
and thrusts me into circulation again.
Alas! the sneering whites scoff,
snort and snivel on my face
as they jingle me about in public.
To them I am still inauthentic,
not worth the dignity God bestowed
upon all his creatures.

When I revalue myself in anger,
the law dumps me in a cell
and out of circulation.

Mother and Child

She sits on the tattered bench,
flashes her thighs as big as a knotted log.
Full of sleep
she nods repeatedly.
Fumes of liquor break out
of her gaping mouth
and chokes her ragged angel.

The child coughs,
frothy mucus erupts from her
nostrils as if they were lava from a volcano.
The baby cries,
bedaubing its sweaty face.
The mother awakes,
barks out her annoyance
with a long scornful face and
wipes off the trembling mucus

She draws her large teats
from beneath her dress
and silences the crying child
that greedily sucks the rich
harvest of its mother's breast
with eyes closed.
Its tiny fingers clawing
the air with joy.

Allan Kolski Horwitz

Between Hammers

Triple Tragedy at Wemmershoek

It was when the clouds were black
on the silver rim of the mountains
that the boy drowned in a sweet-water reservoir —

his father darked
by the slim figure on a diving board;

his mother still on her grandmother's stoep
in the ochre-kloof
where no water ran

near a road junction.

Wired Springboks

Under the trees, red —
yellowing
with auburn, wine-stained leaves,
peddlers
with their boards
of matches and bananas.

Taxis fill with string-bags and iron trunks.

And he who stands on a balcony,
faces the station
where flying springboks
cough blue blood.

As sun-streaks
magnetise the sky,
day is soon night and auburn leaves,
still as the faces of the peddlers,
become black cuts against the springboks
(those ice-blue rings of neon).

He who faces the station has a princess
in bed from the Bamangwato.
Such is the brown of her thongs
that the blood of springboks
reflects and irradiates
her glistening thighs.

He who has a balcony
faces his princess, coasts
his name on her with his lips.

And the peddlers count out change.

Flying springboks irradiate her.

The sky is red and blue;
deep, soft, cosmic
Earth; electric brightening
with dark —
everything above,
built with what's below.

And round the station,
moving with their bundles,
workers board taxis and trains,
hushing children
with the rhythm of their
promises.

The Heads of the World

The heads of the world
compress to a single feature:
a mouth
rich with blood, spittle
and meat.

And a chain of hands
contracted to barren blankets,
the hunter's moon greyed with powdery dumps,
advances the future like a
Zambezi current.

The heads of the world
show their grizzled lip, their leering lip.
Painted or twitching.
Strung, beaded, equatorial lip.
Savaged, open.
Bloody hands clamp bloody mouths:

'Clear corpses, erect monuments, strangle subversion —
become the Rose of Africa.'

For when the East India Company laid gardens
for scurvied sailors
and plotted out a Heerengracht,
did they see the leopard mantle of Chaka
and did they shake?

The heads of the world
compress:
'Encourage foreign investment,
build Cultural Palaces,
arm and strengthen The State.'

In the flaking damp of concrete kraals,
spirit lamps flicker where fires snarled.

And gold-dust chokes the wail
of widowed wives in the Bantustans.
Gold-dust requires
muscular, carbolised, lobotomised
streams from the bush to the compound
passing before the metal detectors,
into and out of, the shafts.

Once the bone-harp of a yellow god
twanged across flamingo lakes,
offered sweet grass,
lush land for milk of cows.
And the heads of the world
would suck and hack the red meat,
rake the fire. And hooves would quicken

as the hard rain of summer
rolled black,
and earth swallowed
the dust clouds of free-ranging beasts.

Hands clamp bloody mouths.
The nightingales of Dimbaza sing,
and the diminutive crosses of the infant dead
cannot bear the sky,
the whistle of women ferrying water.

'Clear corpses, erect monuments, steady inflation.
Become a mouth rich with spittle and meat.
Forget the billowing of sacrificial smoke,
heifers running fat over the full-moon.
Forget the seasons, the chants
of Eternal Life.'

And the heads of the world
compress to a single feature:
a mouth
grizzled, inflamed,
a fissure of the hare-lipped,

rich with blood and words:

our words, our mantle of drills.

State of Struggle

No time, these days
for loitering — (no time)
for indulging the wind.
You come to rest in
a place of incessant action,
hard mountains, too open sky.

You rise each morning with a full day.

No time for (indulging) the wind.

A few weeks ago, you stood
on a beach at night
and the waves were so gentle.
You almost took off your clothes.

Full moon over an unfamiliar city.

Now, inland
there is no such
beautiful ending.

You work.

Vision

Slave and master, pressed
equally, before the stars;

eyes stopped by fists —

some hard and black
with work; others, pale
and soft and powdered —

stopped from bathing
in celestial waves.

Knees knife, bend for the drawing-board.
Slave and master, from dawn,
build huts and palaces.
And predestined astronomers,
known from birth by immaculate signs,

watch the Heavenly Father chain
the Heavenly Mother to his wagon,
saying:

'Pull, woman. Pull me
across these red stars of flame.
Take me steady across
these wastes of sand.

Take me slowly from explosion to explosion.'

And with her womb-like eyes,
she watches him force her down;
she is yoked to his wagon
with her full belly.

And the Heavenly Mother
waters the slaves and their masters
with her open pores.

And then, dreamer, the slaves,
drying their rags on a window-sill,
see a rainbow:

they lift their heads —
she fills the wagon with her light.

Wings

The stoep is light with sunshine.
I take off my shirt.
A black cat crosses the lawn
pouncing on butterflies.
A beetle tips over a leaf.
A washing-machine clicks
into the last stage of its cycle.

In their bedroom,
a man and a woman make love.
He is soundless,
she utters her pleasure.
The cat paws quietly over the grass.

In the kitchen,
servants warm garlic bread,
slice salami;
drop ice into fruit juice.
They lay out a white cloth
on a long wooden table.

The man puts on a record.
The cat arches.
A beetle topples
from the edge of a stone.

I walk to the table.
I eat.
The washing-machine spins.
The black cat blinks
at the yellow-winged butterflies.

He Carries Her

Four times round the world,
the last cockroach bar on the equator,
having taken everything arms, lungs,
veins can take;
there's a pain between his eyes,
between the mind's two hemispheres,
a little back of the brow,
singing too loud in the morning.
Knee-caps shot up, too,
whose scars twitch in fog;
creaking ligaments signal shorter days,
then memory unrolls.

'Purple sunsets in Kruger Park,
gemsbok lapping water.
You stood, lemonade in hand
beside my gin, talking laboriously
of work-force problems.
Then with quick fingers, undressed,
nails reddening my chest,
testing each strand of sandy hair;
craning giraffes at the window.'

He crossed oceans on the decks
of yachts and liners, sleeping in the bowels
where slop-pails filled with peels;
he floated with expensive scum,
a dilettante but useful.
Singapore, Barbados, New York;
washing dishes, washing cars,
washing the sidewalks of butcheries
while working women settled for mince.

'I remember you in Durban
on the Bluff in a borrowed car
(red roofs like linoleum squares,
background to a geometry of cranes).
You pushed your tongue into my mouth
and while hammerheads battered nets,
your fingers, again,
in their authority, found my zip.
(The ocean green, royal-blue,
sea-horses riding south).'

He lies in bed, reads the *Sunday Times*;
drinks warm beer while little girls
jump over rope and their brothers
boot a ball past clothes-lines.
That one woman whom he abandoned,
unknown. Is she dead? That one woman
anonymous now, atoms, so much nameless.

He reads the comics.
Four times around the world, and still,
he carries her single, obliterating
phantom.

Between Hammers

You say:

You speak of freedom.
You commit yourself
to advance.

Arm the masses
with the lanterns
of self-imagination,
LONG MARCH FROM SLAVERY.

While the labyrinth of appetite,
decoys.

The unbridled, the dark;
drunken; muti-murmur; partly
the babble of lies; Manoeuvering
of Interested Vigilantes.
And yet, sometimes, they say,
bullets

turn to water.

Sometimes a striker takes
thirty bullets in the stomach
and survives. Sometimes the same Boere
who come to face us, these same

Blue Boere go down in a surge
of pangas.

They say:

never turn your back
on the Enemy.

Long march from the station
to the Palace of Justice.
Blue Boere and Randlords —
fabric of democracy shredded by their
talons.

But you say
you cannot unmoralise
the whip: puffed face
of the beaten. You say you
will not exclude the beggar,
the whore, the interrogator's
children.

You say your lesson of
Peace and Love:

You preach your sermon — militancy of progress.
The whip, securely licking
the slave's back. The whip,
hungry for muscle, for the slave-woman.
For a Lesson of Peace.

The whip in the hands
of a man who seldom chooses.

And the striker advances
onto the field between the hostel
and the Number One shaft.
He faces thirty-two armed riot police.
And his belly is

the whole field, is thousands of blankets
spattled with the Boers' bullets.

Those who hurl their kierries,
dismissed at negotiations
by the gold price.

The whimpering of impimpi, their sowing of division.
Their fabric of slander.

Now you say you speak

of advancing. You balance
the lies of individuals
against

the lies of organisations.
You judge.

You live in the kernel of intrigue
(cloaked as a play, always a play,
of puffed-up men; straw, they always say —
men in terminal paranoia; balaclava,
Ama-Afrika).

You live in a world of
drying glass.

And the Mine Recruiters
from their villages
suck the men.

They take the village men
and place them in sheds
and take them down as far
as the seams stretch.

These men in the kernel
of nature.

They elect shaft-stewards
and prepare for war. War
on Bobby Godsell with his
unctuous smile of good —
profit.

Scheming librarian, Oppenheimer,
with his sweat-volumes, his accent
of Reason. Chancellor of U.C.T.;
black hats swivel as the
Cartel King

endows a wing for paraplegics.

He sends his
Amabutho —
from the innermost, most high
village in the mountains
(pure traditional river,
long, slow bends in currents of
ripple).

But during the strike, the hostels
under the control of the miners,
the bosses and their private armies
could not enter, or if they did,
it was in fear.

That peasant fist raised to the throat of
scientific digging.

Fool's gold, all of it,
brought up after explosions;
the miners then abandoned

by Jo'burg Head Office —
impressive jangling of phones
to foreign media
but where was the
long-hoped-for, long-dreamt-
of
General Strike of the new-born
Lion, COSATU?

These landless left only
with their hands —
trucked back to the innermost
village —

reeling

with the shock of
dismissal:

Head Office has no answer,
no idea,
no plan of action.

The Corporation that controls
the bellies of Southern Africa,
deprives
fifty thousand families
of their cooking
pots.

And the Lion
yawns.
Till Amabutho
sweep the townships and the hostels
demanding pap
and vleis
and beer, and women:
(they want what's other men's
abundance).

And they axe
the clerk who tries
to hold them back;
they stab the child that cries,
raping his mother.

In the shadow of the Casspir,
their figures lit by burning houses,

the vigilantes drive workers
to war. Another war. An older war.

The Great Indunas still smooth
the hand of the Boer. Gatsha
plots his rival's
grave. (Workers face the Nation).

And, then, a miner
from the innermost village,
anoints himself
with the potion
of maximum power: maximum force in the universe of
ancestral hope.

Thirty bullets in the stomach
but still no Boer can bring him
down. The strike continues, the men
with pangas face death;
bullets drop from the barrels
like drops of water.

And armed with the lanterns
of self-imagination,

we live our freedom.

Commit ourselves to advance:

RATIONAL, COMPASSIONATE.

Push aside three heads, blown heads.
Between them, unspoken alliance
of method.

And historical posturing:

Oppenheimer, Buthelezi and Verwoerd.

The Memory of Freud

In Freud's house, memory
is marshalled
by rows of photographs and vases,
statuettes and writings.

Disciples, enthusiasts, clients of
psychoanalysts
make their pilgrimage to
where the psyche and untrammelled lusts
contend in civilising experiment

(which, amongst other things,
has built this tremor-proof, imperial city;
its palaces and labyrinth).

We ascend the stairs, reflecting
on the inspiration of our loins,
the colours on canvas that delight.

Freud taught to love —

yes, you and I and every passer-by;
the truth above the lie;
the shadow and the blood-burst cry;
the dance of joy and the dance
of the gallows for those who must die;
the flooding of lovers and the curse
of those who have no love but spy;

we need to love one another,
he wrote,

as much as we need our other tools —
our hammers and brushes and drills.

In the toilet at Freud's house in Vienna
(Berggasse — Mountain for Mohammed, for
Moses),
I squat and shit my past meal,
I shit out the cake and cream.
I become the musty dream of Herr Professor
Doktor Freud beneath the parasols
of decadence (O for a line of Papa Doc's
cocaine).

While guards displayed their braid
and helmets with feathers, doctors
of the mind teased out the heat.

But Freud died, removed, exiled
from this city — after eighty years.
Europe's lurch into bestiality,
proof of his analysis. The old man
died in a foreign field.

I have only spent three days in Vienna.
The wealth and solidity of this city
in 1990
is an illusion which is impossible
to deny — try as Marxists
may to uncover the foundation
of tedium and credit and 'guest-workers'

on which it relies.

Will there be another Hitlerite apocalypse?
The past murmurs 'maybe'; the present
opulence sniggers like a hotel manager
ordering his Turkish waiters.

In Freud's house, an uncouth attendant
switches off the lights at 3pm —
get out now, he says:
the streets are yours, the cafes, the shops.
Go, spend. Go wander through our clean streets —
go and eat till you drop.

Engaging Vienna: Mausoleum of kaisers,
gold-plated cathedrals to Christ the Jew-carpenter;
time for poppy-seed tarts soaked in liqueur.

I consider the throw of dice, click of
intrigue, courtly intrigue — the rise and fall
of civilizations:

Let all this buzz in your head.

And when the Minister of Communication
tells you about 'High Definition Television'
on television, on Channel Super

for Europe's youth
(an impressive, intellectual, elegant
Bearer of Mind/Body resolution)

perhaps then you will decide to return
to villages where huts have no electricity
and speak of what you have seen.

Those who consume

are consumed.

Junkie Girl

I looked into the junkie girl's eyes —
compressed, collapsed atoms.
She was in my room.
Junkie girl will do anything
for junk.

I brought her in the early morning,
it was Sunday,
to commune.
No one saw us on the stairs
(I hope).

She sat on my bed,
ran my finger over her junkie lips.
Junkie girl was far,
far,
from the Milky Way.

I asked, 'Are you alright?'
And wondered why I asked.
Junkie girl got up,
took off her clothes,
shivered.

She was thin but not too thin
(not yet).
I licked her brown nipples.
She slowly touched my hair,
my face.

She pulled me down
(oh, baby).
Then curled on my bed,
she lost track, licking
the length of my silver needle.

Far From the Point of Production

The delivery boy packs with expertise;
eggs on top, cans on the bottom.
He shakes a bag and sifts.

She has bought most of the 'specials':
tuna, paper towels, coffee filters,
oranges, chicken breasts.

This week was Andre's turn
but he's away on business.
He has taken five suits —
one for every thousand
he expects in commission.

The delivery boy watches the long, fine hand;
its single gold ring.
She checks the register,
signs a cheque.
Stacked on the counter,
the food is a jumble
of colour and figuration.

There is a mole the size of a small coin
at the side of her neck.
The hairs at the base
are long and fine and scented enough
for someone at his distance
to smell the perfume.

Soon he will see her
in the muted light of a hallway
wearing an Angora sweater.
She will be shoeless.
There will be a table and a cream telephone,
the babble of television.

Then while giving him change,
she will brush his hand
and he will catch, for the first time,
the shaded blue of her scars.

In the North, Past Sabi

He dropped me at Bosbokrand,
a market of soft oranges and over-ripe grapes;
peasant women dumping clusters
into red, plastic bags.
The car, blue with white fins,
a sprinkling of rust round the wheels,
disappears at high speed
(face low, to change tapes).

I squat rolling pips
along the edge of my tongue.
The bush dense at the road-side,
earth thick with ants
hauling the torn fibres of stalks.
And mielies wave
from a far off plateau;
the road stretching —
a thin, black yoyo —
as I wait
for a car to Komaatipoort.

Frank Meintjies

Unclaimed Bodies

Unclaimed bodies

No-one came to claim the bodies.
    Who wants those eyes
    stuck in a moment of fright?
All too scared to touch the
future with its rags, spittle and sand
Scared of that last angry spasm.

Cops with polite words and new names
act as undertakers, stand by to remove bodies.
It's the borrowed balaclava and askari overall
that takes the spattering.

Late at night we crawl with blood on our lips
to the nearest hospital, to the nearest telephone
that's already been ripped from the booth's jaw.

Are we right to measure freedom
by the number of rapes
or by stolen cars that end at cops' feet or by
sparse facilities that we bash up in a groping rage

Are we entitled to measure distance between fitful sleep
and waking with the gavel of the judge
that sculpts the murderer's plea?

The politicians greet us, wave from studio podiums.
The benefit of becoming a nation:
leaders with radiant teeth.
They outline the next step through mikes and wires
celletaped to a reporter's panting chest

The inmates starve themselves
out of the forgotten camps. At the airport
an exile, rummaging for a lost address,
wonders wheretonext

Me, i'm into basic things, no traffic fines
getting washing done on time, finishing things i start
Whisky comforts that i fight for
side by side with those who buy offices at
thirty million rand. It's needed to match the
iron-ball sophistication of the opponent

Who wants to think about dead eyes
— nor balaclavas, shantyclinics and morogo parties?
Neither them, nor I, to claim
the bodies that turn sour and salty in morgues around
Johannesburg

Nightside, Coastal City

High up
the seagulls circle
above fishermen dragging boats
plucking fish from
stringy wetness of gut.
The wind, inconsolable,
shreds the honking and
steelwools on thickened skin

Tall cranes slow-prance
in the ritualistic motion
of the praying mantis.
While at their feet
women, twiglike and robed
in the cheap sparkle of black
slice lean moves through
slurred tongues of wind

The dusktide, slow but dogged,
shovels ashore
piles of flaked shadow
with slurping noises.
In the city centre
the full lights come up:
a fruit bowl of asterisks
and an ink-blotched sky

on blue

when I write
stalking footprints with
net and catapult
look over my shoulder, see myself
following shadows
with splintered eye

when I write I
run my hand over its own shape
run through fields, cities, labyrinths
probing the wind's thoughts
as it trips over skin
purges a stone

when I write
threading time
baked in clay ovens
I lick the sky
smudge the rainbow of an oily puddle

when I write I
set my pen on the sun's bow
arc letters through storm-scrubbed sky
eyes   teeth   nappies   bread sparrows
wired on blue
when I write

you are

you are
you spell yourself out

your footprints
are beads
on wind-chamfered sands
or lost on brackened hills

you are there
a photograph
a word
punched holes on a card

a tracer-line of text, whose peaks and silences
gaze into the thoughts

beyond the seams of your nakedness
you carry a suitcase, a letter from home, a carved stick,
a twig of dried meat
a dustfilm caught just above the lip's dryness

with each ripple of the face
the daily shedding of a million cells
you turn outwards, settle
with the lightness of an insect's shadow
on the wet filament
of the beholder's eye

And Now You Must Go
To Ahmed

The silence of the lone traveller
early for departure,
dips itself
into one last mug of weak tea
the pine bookshelves, loaded with novels
leaning, perchance to hear
the last of your Sevenoak stories
it was sometime between Eid and Christmas

England was calling
just as med school and detention had, and these days
the billiard balls of probablility
on the nuclear physics table

Will those dreaming spires
provide you with forlorn youths to sit around
so you can widen their eyes
with your love of maths?

Britain hangs over you like a fog
it's far from the Ganges and
tambourines that play
by the lean rivers of Africa
symbols your mind wears
as Giant Castle wears its wintercap

You send me pictures of Rookaya and the kids
in anoraks, enjoying a season of familyhood
the detainer's footfall, the weekly call of civic work
lost in a game of snow, or in the pathways of smiles

Three years I have to count the many debates:
is there philosophy in cricket,
or religion in Marxism?
ploughing us through the nights
in the end a mellow tiredness
that you refused to drink to
that left me bundled on the lounge floor

I will summon your jokes, so oft-repeated
with the wetness of your eye
then I will sit and write simple lines
and wonder, with whom
will I now walk through the forests of Cedara?

First impressions
Mishak at one year old

in the beginning was sleep
wrapped in tiny folds of flesh
your blanket a folded handkerchief
of first impressions
that no-one can steal from you
in your pillow the secret
of moulding people from the haze

in the beginning was touch
all seemed drawn to little mouths
your hand designed to find the world
you to judge if
feels and shapes are interesting enough
then you draw us to yourself
to keep forever in the shell of your imagination

in the beginning was a smile
more than the curve of a breastfeeding mouth
in that wrinkle of your face
there's a code that says
hey, i like you
i want to play with you

and the world's a pouch to enfold us both

playing the jack

radio-dj hangs his songs with spit and coke
  beans get second fizz on twoplate stove
    slice leans shiftless from the crusty loaf
      cockroach takes a cheeky daylight stroll
        no hassle here between these draping walls

in the murky water of a cheap coffee mug
  in the rough splay of a wilbur smith
    along the byways of a bemuda couch stroll
      the frayed jack that's flipped and arrayed
        and the square look in the eye:

'i mean
after tying up another helse job
sprucing up the skyline
— kilroy was there, eksê —
a journeyman's got every right
to celebrate
with the lahnies
two hundred grand smile, genuine
hit the brakes, park off
scheme how much I'm worth

hey, I say to the foremen
through the brickie sent to call me
      no time for your hassles
      I'm a top hand
      I'm doing just fine
      on my day 'off sick'

johnny

Teacher bustles through the chapter
how much of square roots did we capture
johnny's called, he sweats and mumbles
words and figures flip and tumble

His ears get hot, his classmates laugh
how much until he's had enough

There's an empty place for johhny gous
apparently he took an overdose

crossbone
aids: minebosses' policy

enclose them in a crate
that will fix their fate
regale them on a plane
gently crash so none remain
secure them in a camp
with skull and crossbone stamp
assign them down a mine
accidents happen all the time

season of the heart

she:
spears dust on a pin of rain
weighs an eye on a cleft-stick
corrodes steel to its membrane
sips the slow-night through a straw

he:
shrouds the houses in a tune
oils the lung of a carnival drum
throws rice in the cauldron
flicks a twinkle in the haystack

together:
they slip a smile through the turret

Rainy Afternoon

The slow rain falls
The solid clouds bump
Like dodgems
Over distant hills
And closer

Wet pieces of
Shattered sky
Drive downwards and slap
the powdery walls

Raindrop fingers
Meticulous
Poke at
The lengthening cracks

Outside like Noah's outcasts
The workers
Press homeward
Hunched forward against the
Blast of icy wind

Uncle Willie tells me
After burying his head in a towel
Then slurping steaming tea:
     No bonus this year.
     You do the work of
     Two. It's a struggle
     Just to keep your job
     These days

Poet

A peristaltic shuffle
up and down against the margin.
Crossing in crossing out, cautiously
toward the right feel.

Scribble on an envelope. Inside
a pressing of words and spaces
shrivels
on a passage to nowhere.

In experimental gardens, a shadow
gives way to a flicker. But, in place
of skewered light — dross and rust
cling to the pen's prodding

The imagination dies at home
and atrophies in exile
The tyrant grins at those
who jest to humour them
The people's poet summons plagiarists
Others measure and cut their coffins
Others, silent, forgotten, gone.

My coat hangs on a rail. Outside
a song and shout
infuses the air.
My feet move to the undercurrent

Inside, I turn pages, have conversations
with my different faces. Only
the masked one has something new:
casually rewriting the stories in my life.
But unlike ex-prisoners and outcasts
I'm too nervous about bluffing.

I bend over my desk. My lines
have the plainness of
potato peels. Words are like veins, far beneath
the skin of laughter.
I work the seams with an apprentice's hands.

I sniff the used up air. Droop.
Commit these stiff moments, today, the next
into the wastepaper bin. Call it a day.

Tomorrow I'll dunk my pen, with renewed zest,
in the soft loam of dry bread and the
flickering eye of sweet black tea. Then
jot down: 'It's starting to thaw.'

first moves
(wino view)

god made the wold
it was duk
like dis bear bottle is duk
then he mayda sky
de river ana sea
and putta fish in
then he saw de mistayk
so he made you an me
and sed
don' say god and poin' to de sky

you de heaven
you and me, we all de sky

Saturday

You are alone for the wake-up
next to a person-shaped space, still
humming with warmth.
Stuyvesant ash grits as
outside, old man sun
with a sparkle on his hoe
pick-and-shovels in the day's energy.

A stolen self-smile
clings to spit and stickiness
lodged in the creases of an unironed mind.
You file and retrieve
that blush, trying to preserve a sample
of that secret aftertaste

You stare at the dressing table
— last night's tilting rock,
in a shadow-sea, rustled by breath-swells
You trace pinboard faces, which enacted
strangers on that distant beach,
eyed you sleepwalking to the water's edge,
returning with glass in hand

Now you slop a coffee breaker
to get the day's orbit
into place. You are a face
in silent ritual of mirror-gazing, still
as the popping of bathtub foam.
Not a grey hair (from what
you can see), only...relief-lines marking
the byways of so many smiles.

cycling home after science class

notions of motion
grain of sand between
fixed patterns and sporadic eruptions
things pushed, heave back with equal force
apples, like all things, to reality's appetite drawn
all loosened, thrown about
no falling overboard allowed

I think on these
as I peddle up against the flexing hill
which muscles back
combusting the sleepy inertia
of classroom science

a poem

let it glide on leather
or 4x4 on sandpaper
towards the sheer edge
of a steel blade pause

so many eyes, coconut white
scooping at the slush of night
so many teeth, tearing the bark
chewing the sinew of the covenant ark

in the crackle of the fusion-pot:
words
buckle twist and then burn bright

Rhythms of Passage

I passed you
astride a Natal roadside
with oranges bright at your feet
a solar puddle,
'john's feet', as they say
marking the field
that blankets forbears' bones
somewhere between
Weza, Ubombo, Harding, Potter's farm
and Vulindlela,
I greet you, so many times
when we meet
in the pupil of a crash-storm
or cursing at a public phone
broken from its moorings
when we are read-out
from between lines and white spaces
between 'Putco eyakho' and 'ngientsha'
we roost on pavements
and under concrete boughs
that shudder
with the anxiety of getting there,
or quivering orgiastically
from the slow-bulking of pantechnikons
our night flickers on pavements
and the surface of cold florals the skin,
then in the cramped bus
cutting through smog
through the silent bowl
of disputed land

tracing escom lines that stop short,
with elementary feelings, we share a lexington
the plaiting of smoke
lean spines on sagging springs,
above the smash and pull
of guitars, pistons, amplifiers
that drum sound
(the echo of our presence)
through layers of time,
that you try to softpedal
with a swearword and a backslap

aftermath

shouts hang from branches
of midnight shadows
night grinds white-eyed in its socket

still the throat lumps
with swallowing action
suitable for dashing of spit and blood

under pulsing eyelids
shadows of thrust, lunge, parry
procreate, close in
over walls and all that moves

finally
a cigarrette smoulders
into bullets of smoke that pierce the eye

the silt of cooled perspiration
gathers
in catchment valleys
far beyond the eye's pulsed batting
and solitary sightprints

the flint of your anger
recedes into
the supple paw of silence

meeting place

at the meeting place
at the rendezvous
our bodies shall curve
in winds of lust

we'll paint
colours on the tongue
turn paddling breath to oars
propelling us
into a cauldron of surrender and self-interest
        and in the whalebelly
        of this season the lovers' music
        sprouts an ivy of sound

each leaf's rustling
breaks somewhere in the distance
and like gnats to a windscreen
we hurtle
into the purple iris
where the night incubates
making us over with every pulse

one-an-other

the new s.a.
        one lying on a park bench, other sitting up
        one crying from the sting, other crying foul
        one sits on millions, other sitting in
        one persuing the other, other on the run
        one buying the school, other has no books
        one agrees, other has no tongue
we are one

Counter Number Five

The women in the floral blue-green
is counter number five. My words do a
weary-moth slapping
against the double-thickness of
safety glass
whipping juice of open-mouths
to the texture of candledrip

She shouts that I should
speak up. I do, but my open mouth's ideal
for her favourite stuffing: don't get
cheeky with me!
The rubber stamp, silent
and patient as a chess piece,
looks at me. I give the humble eye
and pass the thin slices of paper.
She glances at icinged lips
in the mirror's extension
before thumping my photo
with a loud bang.

In the double thick glass
I see my neck, browned
as the crust of dark bread.
And blushing a little,
note how over-tropical
the lashings
of my orange-green shirt.

The Taste of Jo'burg

The bones, firm and rutted,
draped with organisms. Stirring
that special kind of froth.
A sunset glow
on shoulders of a mine dump.
Neon spires
that never sleep.
Shrewd rats, nesting in shoes
and in bolt-holes of armpits
waiting for the right moment.

Lying down, legs astride and
feet in the gutter, from where
soft eyes passing, turn away.
The wrinkled parts.
And mouth-soft words
lie tipped in the gutter
beside Chesterfield butts.
Near orange-bannered cafes
cooking in smells,
shekels of blood
track pavement-scents
to the lair of tenements.
Garbage alleyways crouch
in the piss-stain of a shadow.
Here the imports — electrified
names from great capitals.
There the tooth-smile of cardin,
and a mouthfull of jewels.

I greet with a tinkle
and a smile from the billboards
I/you/we in passing by
handprint a grubby note

No lipice breath
          of a southeaster
No curry-scent
          on a salted breeze

johannesburg city, unmistakable froth

girl with the maroon hat

my beloved is tired
she needs some sleep
she drinks glass after glass of wine

she looks enthusiastically
into the windows of my eyes
sees a girl
with maroon hat
dancing and dancing
under a plain white ceiling and the glow of a lightbulb
to slump into a weary bundle

everywhere, the
girl with the maroon hat and a smile follows her
into the bedroom
swivelling
into the quiet corners of my armpit

the swirl of the dance
the unpleating of the skirt
sits in the eye like an inappropriate colour
or an unwelcome speck

my beloved is tired
she needs some sleep
away from my eyes' reflectiveness
she needs to talk to the girl
now circling the piano
to touch the sensual strangeness of that dance

jackhammers

i have no rueful smile
to ask this moment's pardon
no rudder-tongue words
to flutter from the softness of my mouth

only jackhammers
to break the walls of this house

lovely road

love for your country will keep you
but love for your children lets you go
— Alan Paton

the lovely road runs
from Carisbrooke to Ixopo
through twig-snapping foothills of
mission schools and vast lands
scaffolded with bible verses
and heavy bookshelves

the road is sorry
about the callouses
of those who know it
from the barefoot eye-view,
but (as they say in inquests)
no one is responsible,
when the sleek wheels of history
outrun those
with outmoded rituals
and no voting experience

the quaint sash of tarmac
flanked by grass that is holier than tar
exhorts that we should give
yet another chance
six months times six months
to yet another tyrant

the road's hot river bed
where insects drone
has a subdued pensiveness
in strong dissent with those
whose feet flail and stamp
in the open-air
raising the stakes
— the road calls for peace
the poignancy of hymns
the organ strains of contemplation

the lovely road
snug as a sun-warmed centipede
does not reach logical conclusions
becomes a twisted cufflinked limb
       touching airports and bonzai conferences
       paved with scenario books:
       whitehaired, moving announcements
       but no departure or take off
       from plains of responsibility

there is another road
from the location to Pretoria

a damp season

it's a damp season
where the steady dripping
wedges fluid between the grains
and everything heaves
to a beat of awakening and decay
and the doors won't shut because the sky is swollen
and the expanded weight shifts
in the tightness of stretched nylon

it's a damp season
of hunched shoulders
and a trickle behind the ear
and a drop pushing past eyelash
when trees are heavy
and bark waits and waits to peel back
while sleep in short shifts
nestles in folds of
wet cloth that clings to skin

it's a damp season
of nightlight broken into myriad facets
and daylight murky and feeble
with incessant sloshing
in the cracked pipes of the edifice
and the gargle of a broken toilet, in chorus
with the smoky sputter of a fire
under grey broth that streaks the saucepan

indeed, it's a damp season
serote's dry white season dry as wire
has given way. It's a time
of drenched roots and sodden buds
in creviced and windblown gutters
that holds sway

Lisa Combrinck

The Shadow of Desire

Those who restrain desire, do so because theirs is weak enough to be restrained; and the restrainer or reason usurps its place and governs the unwilling.

And being restrain'd, it by degrees becomes passive, till it is only the shadow of desire.

— William Blake
'The Marriage of Heaven and Hell'

I Write

I write:
your lips are slices of bread
your tongue is a piece of meat
your body is a rock shining like the sea
your eyes like dark coals warm me

your body is a blanket
which covers me

you are a gift
and I wrap myself around you
like a creased sheet

but it is no use,
these simple phrases do not help me

my love for you
must shine in primary colours,
fill banners
and the smallest squares with colour

my love for you
must clad the world
in new clothing, bright colours,
precious metals, rich harvests

my love for you
must be dressed like a carnival
of ferris-wheels and swings

Freedom

He danced naked in the forbidden garden.
His body glowed in the sun.
The leaves like waving dancers stroked his body.
He danced, fulfilling himself
with the rich, curving ripeness of the fruit.

Dizzy with desire, he lay down to rest in the greenery.
The grass caressed him.
The wind watched over him.

He felt it in him and around him.
The mouth of the river washed him.
The tongues of grass dried him.
The wind sang to him.

He arose again to taste this life again
to feel the fulfilment of the fruit.
His eyes were coals of insatiable desire.
He could not sleep.
He ate more of the fruit.
His needs could not be satisfied.

Greedy with desire, he went from tree to tree,
gluttonously devouring the fruit. He tasted every fruit,
until he could not distinguish one taste from the other,
until his body
was stained all over with the blood of fruits,
until the garden was a confusion of entangled branches,
a devastation of colour.
The paths strewn with rotting fruit.

Satisfied, he lay down to rest.
His body was tired and worn out.
He lay his head down on the bloodstained ground.
Before he shut his eyes he saw
the garden, reproducing new fruit.
He stared in disbelief at the fruit,
more beautiful, more succulent than he had eaten.
But too tired, he could not move.
And fell into a deep sleep.

He awoke to the hardness of stone
beneath his body. He rose to see a landscape
of sand and stones.
He ran across the stony plains,
thinking he had lost his way.
He searched for the garden. But found only
a barren greyness, stretching on all sides of him.

Then, his body sore,
his feet aching from the sharp stones,
he flung himself on the ground in misery and loneliness.
He shouted in despair: 'Who are you?
Why have you left me?'
His voice was wild,
then pleading, becoming faint and incoherent.

He was answered in a thundering, shrill tone.
He could not see the form behind the blinding glare.
He could only feel and hear the throbbing voice,
going back and forth, back and forth,
through his shaking, fearful body. As he came,
in the violence, his consciousness returned.

A woman replied:
'I am freedom that you want to warm you.
I give you now what you gave me.
I leave you with nothing like you left me.
I am freedom and not faithfulness.'

The voice left him abruptly.
He felt confused and alone.
He stood spellbound, until in puzzlement
his body turned to stone. His eyes frozen in desire.

A Man

the poem
is a worldmap

my muse
is a man

he walks the world
tall   proud   stripped of light

sometimes I hide in the shadows
and wait for the coming of night

he overpowers me
then vanishes from my sight

my muse
is just a ruse

the world map
is a growing gap

and the poem
is a hole

through which an arrow passes.

Women

the poem
is a veil

the word
is the woman

behind the veil
her lips part slowly

she wants to speak
but she doesn't know how

so she shuts her mouth
the veil disappears

a poem dies
before it is born.

I Want to Build You a House

I want to build you a house
made from my arms

I want to make you a bed
in my lap to rest your head

and the breeze blowing through the house
will be my hands brushing your hair as you sleep

and the world will be as warm as the oneness of a hug
and as strong as our embracing arms

and we shall breathe songs as we sleep
and make poems without speech

what more could we ask for
but lullabies of love

and to wake up with the delicate dawn
smiling in our eyes.

The Problem With Words

The problem with words
is that they weaken us,
they imprison our love
like print on a page.

The problem with words
is that alone they are meaningless.
Words should be wooed to action.

When I whisper words to you:
only if the sounds finger your skin,
only if they stir your spirit deep within,
only then are they true.

Sex is Sweet

After Stephen Crane

Do not weep, maiden, for sex is sweet.
Love comes in a capsule, inserted quick.
Coupled with a rubber bag which unravels
And rolls on at the right time.
Do not weep.
Sex is sweet.

Because your lover loves you, wants you,
And your loins throb fiercer than your heart

There is enough spring in the bed
For your rhythmic communion to go ahead

As planned, or pre-planned in pills
Taken day by day.

So, do not hesitate, begin the play.

As you tumble together between the trembling sheets,
Touch after touch, kiss after kiss, skin shaving skin,
And finally love comes in.

So what if your dream died then.
And your body shed blood.
Do not weep.
Sex is sweet.

The Journey

My love
you have lost your way

put your finger deep within me
return to the source
and confirm your route

the spoors of struggle
are difficult to identify
and dangerous to follow

do not be afraid
do not fear defeat

we have opened the road for you
petal after petal lies strewn along the route
like unfurling flags flying freely

I feel your eager prints on my body
moistening the present
mapping out the future

my love
reach out into the darkness

trace the origin of the sweet scent of desire
feel that freedom begins as a fire
flowing and filling the passages of power

Concerning the Subject Matter of This Poetry

It so happens that I am tired of being simply a person
in the political melting-pot.

I am weary of weaving words
into another torn, tattered tapestry of the times
we live in, the tedium of producing political patches,
the piecemeal records of events,
impoverishing our political struggle
by aborting all talk of sex.

It so happens that I want to be a woman undeniably
who writes erotic love poetry.

I declare emphatically for you and all the world to see
that I shall sing openly and honestly of sexual love.

I shall sing proudly
about being a woman.

Write about the love of a woman
for a man

Through the lips of a woman
and not through a man.

Finally, if nothing else:
to let the poem throb furiously
with an urgent, persistent femininity.

To the Reader

Why should a woman not write erotic love poems?
It is true that most of my poems are about the struggle:
shaping words into the stones we throw at the
                                        oppressor,
shaping words into the slogans we shout;
shaping words into salve-covered swabs to heal our
                                        wounds,
shaping words into spears with which to forge ahead.

But these cold stones, these slogans of struggle,
these wounds, these spears cannot be free
until they come to terms with femininity
and feel the freedom of love.

No one is in love with the struggle.
We fight for the rights of people
to have land and love. We lose our lives
to liberate those we love.

In this struggle, let us leave some space
for people to love, love's bleeding lips, a blushing face.

And allow this woman the right unconditionally
to write lines and lines of erotic love poetry.

Life Cycle

I am writing this poem about the deaths
of a little boy, Pedro Page,
a young mother, Liziwe Masokanye,
a mother-to-be, Yvette Otto,
and all the other children
and men and women who were killed
on the night of the elections.

I do not want to write this poem. I plead with myself.
Because when you write a poem about death,
something inside the poem dies.

I justify my actions by saying
the poem will be a tribute to the lives
of those who have died.
But this justification is not enough.
The lines of this poem linger and lengthen and something
inside stiffens and dies.

Strong statements lose all meaning.
And I ask myself endless existential questions:
How many more poems will we have to write
about those who have died?
How many more meaningless deaths, how many more
callous crimes have to be translated into poetry?

In the week of the elections, so much blood was shed.
In Khayelitsha, Kalksteenfontein, Kleinvlei, Mitchells Plain,
Kaya Mandi — in so many living suburbs
of our city, the young and the old, but mostly
young people, were shot to death
— and nothing this poem can say
will bring any one of them back.

After the deaths and the maiming of the young,
there were vigils and funerals
to bury our dead. And there will be more
vigils and funerals, tributes and elegies
to those who have died and will die.

We shall have words that wail and weep on the page
as death is dictated line by line,
woeful word after word, until the words of the poem lie
birdshot buckshot bullet-ridden on the stained page.

The structure of this poem is the length and breadth
of the struggle. A road etched in pain.
The shape of the street on which young people are killed.
Are these words nothing more but a product
of the destruction of people?

And a voice inside the poet cries out against the terror:
I want to write about life....
I want to celebrate living, life and love....
I no longer want to write about death. Like a coward,
I shirk at this responsibility.

I want to write about those who at this moment
are being conceived,
about the babies who are being born right now,
and about those who are yet to come.

My lips breathe life onto the page.
A throbbing, pulsating, earthy life.
The sounds now soften. They speak
of love on summer nights.

And so the poet wallows in love and life,
floats in the passion of pure emotion,
asserts the humanity of people.

The poet pauses awhile to fashion pregnant phrases,
to search for sounds to mimic the making of love.

We shall have words that make love on the page,
phrases that cling to one another inseparably yet carefree,
and stanzas that sing so completely from the soul
of the joys of life, love, labour, and of the rising sun.

Then, somewhere in the night, two shots ring out.
They provoke the poet into unbearable pain and suffering.
Two tears of blood drop onto the page.
The blood of death and the blood of birth
now seem simultaneously one.

Words

I want my words
to be as simple
as bread
as water
and as love

but the bread
becomes green with mould
the water
dark and stagnant
and love
loses its lustre.

Peter Anderson

If I Shut My Eyes

Key to the Kingdom

The child has laughing dark eyes,
And a shy way of putting her head
On the shoulder of the worried
Rescue worker, who tries to explain
To camera
That the mother is dead, the father is dead,
The gunmen unknown, but they shot up the party,
The Christmas party, the same night I
Was at Carols by Candlelight in the park
With my children on my knees,
And my wife said to me:
'It takes you back to your childhood, doesn't it?'
As the Salvation Army raised their splendid brass
In the rain, behind them the lake
Brilliant and dark with the lights shaking across it,
And the minister who strangely had
Exactly my name
Proclaimed through the whoop and whistle
Of a microphone
That the child in us held the key,
The key to the kingdom,
And if only we would kneel with him
There and repent right then,
He would guarantee us all
Peace on earth and goodwill to men.
But the child in me looks now at the child
With gleaming eyes whose parents have been shot
By 'unknown assailants',
And I know now Christ was no better than this child,
And this world shall be changed for her sake.

King Kong's Skull

There are three young men in the street.
It keeps growing darker and darker,
Cars come down the street.
Streetlights flick on. The old retired Greek
Cafe owner won't leave his post
At the upper window. You can see
The glow of his cigarette, intense
As he draws on it. And I, outside
Where I can smell the earth after rain,
And looking up can see the sky green
And mild as a holy river,
With dark clouds massed in it like islands,
I, too, am glad to stay and watch

The young men's game of catch. Throwing
A frisbee — an orange wobbling skimming
Plastic high-flyer — lobbing it,
Sending it spinning, they pursue it
Among parked cars in the narrow street,
Leap up with a shout, a laugh,
And catch it or miss it —
Alive to one another, casual,
Strong.

                    And I remember
The Skeleton Song
In Todd Matshikiza's King Kong
When I was a child — how
The skeleton danced,
Stripping himself

Of all his bones
Until he was nothing but
A green skull
Glowing and
Jiggling,
Laughing
At darkness.
Then he tossed away
His head, too,
And the dark
Went dancing
On the dark.

The frisbee goes floating,
Spinning, and lands,
And somebody scoops it up.
It sails my way,
And I collect it, hold it a moment —
A luminous thin-spun plastic disc:
I can see my fingers through it
Like an X-ray — shining,
Before I send it curving high in a loop,

Flaring faintly, like a comet,
And the next guy gets it,
And the next. No one can stop.

King Kong's skull is shining in the dark.

The House Arrest of a Private Man

In the slack afterdinner collapse of the lounge,
It's TV News at Eight. Through a streaming windscreen's
Boxed-in crouch, a road sign
Flaps slantwise
In a wind that can't
Be heard:

NO ENTRY

Aerial shots of flooded towns, waters still as a dam
Turning clockwise as the plane banks,
Roofs of the suburb like rafts,
Full-foliaged trees half under,
A van on a bridge
Looking badly humbled:
'Three tornadoes hit this state
Together — a world record!'
The torrent churning.

Down Main Street now
Comes blurring a motorboat,
Steered by this grim old guy
In a red peaked baseball cap
Under a sky of cloud
That hangs soft low and like walls
With the rain still drifting down.
                    I switch off —
The clutter inside me yet
Of shots cut together rapidly, shakily,
With the maximum hysteria,
Urgency and hype.

                    Outside my window,
Under a moon that stands quite clear and still,
An iron hippo lands up stuck
With a grunt of gears then silence.
Tarmac glistens. Figures flat as targets
Dismount. I distinctly
Hear a young soldier say, 'Shit!'
I half-hallucinate the souls of the dead,
Lean my head on the glass:
It is instantly sweaty to the touch.

I envy America its new world record.

Eel

Behind bullet-proof glass
Underground
In this dank and sweating tank
Of an aquarium,
Misty seawater puffs green and tepid,
Toxic-looking as trench gas.

There's nothing else in the weird gloom
But I stay awhile
And shiver: the shadow
Of a hammerhead, a sea turtle's
Muddy flipper. Then, under a ton

Of bulging brain coral, I see —
Panting and pulsing
And as broad as my chest —
A tropical eel, doubled
Up. Its hide is canary yellow,
A pincushion
Of black dots. Its eyes,
Little waxen beads, seem tinier
Even than its leopard
Spots. It can surely not

Pick me out, but
I press my face flat
Against solid glass
And sweep my hands around
As though I'm slipping
And this is my S.O.S.

The eel only pumps and smiles,
Pumps and smiles and sucks.

It gulps as greedily at water
As an old man, dying, whose
Shrunken mouth stretches
At air and gags
On itself, lips purple
And rolled back, thin.

Its bite would deliver an electric shock.

After Amanzimtoti

I remember nothing of this barren and hot
Little seaside resort,
Save the pavements and the heat.

My father in a two-tone safari suit,
Sweat glistening on the roll of fat
Behind his head,
Butting his way boisterously
Out of the pub
After eight beers.
'Come out and fight!'
Putting both fists up playfully
To my mother
And backpedalling
On the tarmac
Like a boxer,
While I sat close beside her
In the airless black Ford
In the mounting heat,
As she crushed
A small handkerchief
Tight in her palm
And pressed it
Carefully
To the edges
Of her eyes,
And muttered
In her mortification: 'I've had enough.
I'm fed up to here.'
Pointing to her throat.
'I couldn't care!'

A small handkerchief with
Red dots. It smelt
Of perfume, I remember. I held it
Fluttering out of the window
And lost it
When we got out of there —
Lurching triumphantly from one side
Of the road to the other —

In the hills
Beyond the town,

Amanzimtoti.

Where a bomb blast now has smashed a shopping centre
I never saw. Killing five. Maiming for life
I don't know how many.

           And at night,
I dream of my long-dead mother.
Mother, I say, mother,
It must be here somewhere.

I'll find it yet,
Small and white with little red dots
And perfume (cheap stuff),
I remember — if I have to dig
Through every bit
Of shattered glass,
And move these mounds of dumped brick
(I've swallowed dust, I'm shaky)
Down to the sea's sticky edge

Where birds with sharp beaks are pecking at something
Under long split twists of chrome
Which weigh on me.
Though the man with the flap of blood for a face
Tugs at my sleeve
And tries to deter me, while I
Pick up the hand
Of the toppled shopwindow dummy
With the bald head and dolly-bird eyes,
Whose lips whisper to me
Of the tick of sand in the glass
Where the sea floats away my guts,

Mother. How could I forget?

Are the hills
Where the dead live
Green and lush, and

How are you really,
Mother?

Don't stay too long.

Your griefstricken son.

If I Shut My Eyes

We are a new generation. We are not afraid to die.
— Township youth.

Often enough, I've imagined my own funeral
All heaps
Of creamy magnolias smothering
The coffin —
Itself a magnificent
Piece of furniture —
And the smell
Beginning,
And a single blundering
Fly,
Who despises everything but funerals,
Alighting
On my bony forehead. Then, too,
The tannies
In their special church hats,
Crying
(The dried-up sanctimonious cows)
Or peeping through their fingers
In suffering, and
Trying to figure the costs.
The minister's pronouncements
Full
Of anguish as he tries to calm
The congregation down
With promises deader even
Than I am
From his pulpit in the suburbs.
And the hot red earth

Where they lay me,
Finally, to boil
In the dark.

So much for me.

Sunday. Today, in Kwa-Thema, New Brighton,
Tembisa, Winterveld, Alexandra, KTC,
They are burying the dead. I know.
But can think of it only
With disbelief. And dread.
I could smash my head
Against the wall and cry out to God,
If the only answer weren't this ringing
Emptiness. Stupor. Placidity
Of my neighbour, watering her lawn.

I see the parched scuffed grass
And dustbowl
Of a stadium like Orlando,
Where red, or black, green and gold
Flags lie draped across the cheap
And blatant coffins. No flowers,
Except one plastic 'everlasting' wreath,
And girls like bridesmaids
In little veils and elbow-length gloves
Who stand at intervals
Along the rows of the dead.
The grandstand is choked to capacity.
'VIVA!' The crowd surges.
Banners unfurl. While through
The echoing ricochet

Of loudspeakers,
orators affirm

That the people *shall* govern.
And even the sweating priest
Lead the masses in hymns
To freedom. As, gaunt, the swollen-faced
Comrades shoulder and carry the coffins,
And strike at the sky with their fists:

I think. I imagine.

Here in my room,
The bed stiff and comfortless with its spread of
              newspapers.
if I shut my eyes,
I'm stifled.

A child's kite
Cut out of newspaper,
Hovers over a rutted
Township street somewhere,
Capsizes,
Loops head over heels
And dives
Right under the wheels
Of a Casspir
As the killers roll in.

I know, if I could see
My own coffin
In the middle of a stadium
And the thousands outnumbering death,
Surging for life: 'Viva!'
I would scrabble for stones, too,
As the children do.

But since I am who I am,
All I really see is this ragged nameless body
Crushed and lying huddled in the street,
With a few sheets of newspaper
Half over it. And a face
Already gathering flies.

Return to King's Square

I am twenty years too late and there is no
Going back, but I make my way
Across the park where willows which once
Hung frail in collars of iron
Have sprung up thick and strong
Beneath the giant immobile clouds
This afternoon, trailing green and golden
Chains whose tips just brush the heavy waves
Of grass. Beneath the closest willow, I once
Made love. In the dark — my hands
Blindly touching her face, her hair.
My denim jacket hastily doubled
Under her, her legs jack-knifed up.
She whimpered my name. It traps me now

To think of it. Of her. Sandy?
Cindy? Gone I don't know where.

And back farther yet, I used to play
Here when it was plain old King's Square,
All emptiness and dead dry veld grass,
And in the middle,
Mud in the mouths of twin great
Stormwater drains
That flooded the place in summer,
The rest of the time stood stagnant,
A mosquitoes' swamp or paradise.
A boy my age got drowned there once.
They pulled him out, his small limbs
Angled stiffly, soaked shirt
And short pants
Clinging, and wrapped him in
A blanket on a narrow
Stretcher. The sunken square
Was flat with water, rain still falling,
I remember. The whole neighbourhood
Was there, led by five
Young policemen in capes, waving weak
Torches. A frogman
Pulled him out. Black-goggled
And flippered, he stood there gaping,
Afterward, as if he only now could know
What he had groped at in the flood.

'And you, don't you ever go play
In the tunnels again,' my parents warned.
But armed with matches, rope
And flippers, although the first tunnel
I set foot in was dry as dust
And the draught blew thick and dark,
Catching my throat, I disappeared down it. No star
Of daylight twinkled at the end.
There's our house at last, the tame
Yellowbrick. Behind it,
The railway line, as always. And,
As if caught in the hanging cables,
The cross of the church.
Our stoep's the same, I see. Black polish,
Slippery when wet. But will my mother
Open the door and curse at me,
Shaking her fist? I half expect it. Ma,
The strawberry blonde, wobbly fat, her eyes
Tarted up to bring out the blue,
Eyebrows plucked and pencilled,
How long ago was it? And Pa,
His sleeves rolled up to show his biceps,
Face swollen like a bulifrog's,
Will he sing his party piece:

> 'A-ah, sweet mystery of life,
> At last I've found thee....'?

Strangers have painted the gate. I turn aside,
Cross the street. It is twenty years too late.

Lubavitch Lady With Pram

She crosses the road toward me
Breasts milk-plump and swinging,
Tight-spun wig askew, showing me
An edge of her real red hair,

Bumps the pram's wheels
Against the kerb and jolts
The contraption
Up. Her fine white fingers

Are tense: I'd like to untense
Them. I'd like to pop them
Into my mouth and suck them, one
By one, and not only them —

But a line between her brows
Divides us as sharply as if
To say: 'Get out of my way. I don't
Know you.' And I, like Abraham

In the wilderness, ragged, mad
And hollow with God, think: 'Fuck!
It's true. I'd give
My foreskin to get to know you.'

A Problem With Doors

I never believe they will open quite right.

The handle will stick.
Or the click I get will be only half latch,
Half safety catch
As some Rambo from Z-Squad
Picks his teeth, ready
To tickle the trigger
Of his all-purpose Uzi
And drill me just as I
Step in. I can imagine

How I'll fall — my blood
A surprise too slippery
To be plugged by my fingers —
How I'll kneel on the floor
And stare. It's ridiculous.

Doors have lost their innocence.

On top of it all, everywhere
There are doors.
(Most of them locked.)

As for trying to knock,
It's like that picture
I once saw
Of Jesus — King Jesus,
His head
With its blood drops

And bush of thorns
Tilted
At the angle
That indicates
Doubt — in one hand, a lantern,
The other hand
Raised
To knock. And beneath him
The legend:
'Love LA LA LA'
Or something. Except, I'm not
Jesus. And anyway, it's useless to knock.

It's getting so heavy that even my sleep
Is populated with doors. I dream
They fall shut while I stiffen
(Or part of me does). Then I roll over
And pitch
Down the bottomless
Well. An iron lid
Groans. I am faintly aware
Of distant helpless hammerings,
Thin screams. And at my heels, struggling
And panting like a dog, flops
The hangman's black bag without
The hangman in it. Or I'm back
In the long dim corridor of some sweaty hotel
Of my childhood. It smells of stale beer,
And a puddle keeps growing
Under the door whose number
I can't quite make out. And I wake up
Cold with knowing that the wet sheet
Under me is the precipitate of pure fright.

My next step might logically be
To attack a door and rip it
Off its hinges —
But what if the posts
Were to sprout
A double row of nails,
Ready to snap
Like some Mediaeval trap?

No. The most I can do is scrawl
On the face of the nearest door:
        HELP!
WHO KILLED DULCIE SEPTEMBER?
R.I.P. RICK TURNER
DANGER   GEVAAR   INGOZI

I seem to see the long slow burst
Of the detonation — the first
Bright wavering light. I feel
That sense of heavy numbed limbs
Planted, going nowhere,
And the terrible ripping shock.

And I think of you, Albie Sachs.

On a lovely day of high blue sky,
Tumbling clouds and the sea — a holiday
If ever there was one — you crossed
The streets of the old colonial quarter
And stopped beside your car to look about you
And breathe. Then you slipped
The key into the lock
And triggered the explosion
That tore off your arm
And left you on your back
In the street, struggling to get up

And in that endless instant,
Fully conscious.

While I curl up
Tight in my corner
And rock
And beat my head
As though a hole in the wall
Were the only way out,
And anyway, it is all just
My own paranoia —

A problem
With doors.

Zoo/Noose

A massive muscle-bound bullet-headed
Gorilla has shat in the overripe
Chopped-up pawpaw of his lunch,
And now sits pressing one
Gnarled finger curiously
Into pawpaw and shit and smelling it
With a certain profundity: his sunken chest
Heaves as he squats in a corner of the cage,
The ponderous philosopher.

On an open
Perch
An orange and blue
Macaw
Idiotically,
Craftily cries: 'Hello!
Who, who? How are you?'
And mumbles lewd things
To herself in the sun, scratching her chin
With a foot grey and shrivelled
As a mummy's.

To my right, a glass window looks empty
Except for my own reflection. I cup
My hands around my eyes and lean up
Close. Make out a mound
Of pythons in a slump
Waistdeep, not stirring. And a little
White mouse,
A leftover from lunch,

I think —
Inquisitive, skittering around,
On edge. Sometimes it stands on
Hindlegs like a kangaroo,
And sniffs, quivering, as if
For a way out. I can't watch.

I go on. Sweating and smiling in the crowd
In the sun. I wear a peaked cap
Without a crown and for fun
Hold up a plastic windmill
That won't spin even when I blow.

Past the tigers. Where the male,
Shut in behind an iron gate,
Moans his agony to his mate
On heat. While she twists round on her back,
A smile on her face,
Twists round and toys with a blade of grass.

As bad as the brown bear,
Or almost — a big guy,

Alone in his pit, who rocks
And sways and swings his square head,
Banging it against the wall,
Bored and insane and far too tame. I toss him
An empty peanut shell.

Then up stone steps again
I find myself round the back
Of the cages
Where the goats are kept
For fresh meat. They stare
Right through me,
Chewing at the straw of a scattered bale.

There is nowhere to go now but back.

In a corner where I've never been
Before, I stop
And watch five or six lean-bellied
Wolves with bushy tails
Trot up and down
On legs like twigs.
They won't meet my eyes. Then one,
A bitch, squats as if to pee
But howls. I am
Screwed by the sound. A wolf
Myself, I run,

I run. In search
Of the snow that is nowhere. With the fence
Wound tight round my throat.

'Nkosi Sikelel' iAfrika...'

This dreary battered and sad old hymn
Smells to me of paraffin,
Stoep polish in a dented
Tin, a primus stove
Like a squat
Brass king, a bar
Of blue soap, flat
And thin, wedged between teeth
Of a scrubbing brush rubbed
Almost to the gum, late
Afternoon sun, a small
Backyard room,

And Anna. Her bed
On its stilts of brick, for fear
Of a little man,
The tokolosh' — only
About as high as I was
Then — with a terrible grin
And a standing prick, who
At any time
Might walk in. As I did, too.
To press my face between her breasts
And smell the skin,
Or pluck at her blouse
Until she smiled
And undid
The last big button
To let me suck,
And I could sleep high

On the hard bed, and
She left. ('Fired! Out
Of the blue!' Pa grinned at me
And wagged his finger. 'You
Think I didn't know
What she was up to with you?')

Hillbrow Street Scene

The dogs' fur looks glossy, bristling,
Cushy as bedding, crammed against the cop car's
Wire grille. They choke
On their own saliva, rave
And snarl, ready
To tear your throat out if
You stick so much as
A little finger through the wire.

                    Two young cops
Hang round the driver's door,
Sleepy, pallid — faces shut. It is long
Past midnight. The tall one murmurs
What might be lovetalk
Into a mike while the dashboard
Radio buzzes and blurts: 'Hallo, Jannie! Sê my, waar
Is julle?' And strobe
Lights on their swank
Yank squad car swing round and round,
Blue and red, flooding us all
With hell light.

On the pavement,
Curled on his side,
The now dead young man lies,
Both eyes wide
As though spellbound
By the silence
Holding him down to the ground.

I've got to get out. I shove my way
Sideways through the crowd. And yet
I take advantage of the crush
To press up close
To a fat black whore in tight
Black jeans, and tug
At her zip — which splits
Half open. She scowls
in my face, earrings
Jingling, 'Hai! Voetsek.'
Hot liquor on her breath.
A heavy, lipstick-rich big mouth.
'Okay?' I say. And she nods, fixing
Her fly. Our fingers link.
Nobody notices.

We cross the street together,
Arguing softly about price. On the pavement huddles
My shadow like a cut-down
Cut-out of myself. I step
Aside. Squeeze her hand. Forget that.

Item For a Killer

I used to think a stocking
Would be better. It smears your face
Into such a mess, a bloodless
Abortion, a horror
Comic, a spook. But this
Simple thing,
A black balaclava,
Unfolds so neatly,
Softly, in my hands:
I try it on.

Snug enough to be itchy,
It clasps my face, tight
Springy wool
Closing over my nose:
I feel mysterious,
More unknown than warm.
Fine moisture from my breathing
Dampens an area. I open my mouth —
It forms like a hollow in a sock.
In the mirror, my eyes glint sidelong.
(Who am I? No one could
Tell.) Killer, I see what you
Need. If the cold could cut
To the bone,

And you don't want to bleed.

Letter to Mandela

I don't know you, father. But you are
My father. I have not forgotten.
It has been very long. Almost
A lifetime. A lifetime
Like death
Behind the iron gates.

I would like to touch
You, father. For something
Like wisdom
Might come to me through
My fingertips.
I would like to hear your voice,
My father. All my life
I have been bereft.
I have sought for you
In people's faces
In countless places.

❖

I am the man who rides the lift
Late at night. Tired,
Crushed in the throat. Ten
Floors, twelve floors up —

Floor after floor, the still yellow light
And the shut steel door making
Almost a cell. Paint scratched
And peeling. Smelling faintly
Of piss. It stops
And the numbers blink red:

And in steps the night cleaner,
Mrs Maponya, a shrivelled
Old bit of mischief
Only elbow high, with a glint
In her eye,
And a bucket and broom.
'Eh, ma!' I complain. 'I am finished.'
She wants to know why, but I shrug
And lie: 'Work.'
And she grins at me with her only tooth.
'Work!' she scolds happily. 'My son.
It makes you strong.'

✦

I write you a letter, my father.

I should have written before.
All night in my room
High above the city, I write:

'You are the storm
That leaves the street smoking
And I
The gap-toothed child
Who runs, steering
A long prod of wire
With a buckled wheel
Past the burnt-out hulk
Of the armoured car
With grass spurting up
Through its seams
Like wildfire.'

The shiny black panes
Of my window
Are slowly dissolving,
Becoming light
By the time
I take the lift
Down again
To street-level.

Let the gulls scream
As they reel and swing
Round the walls between
Us today, too, then,
My father. It will not
Always be so.

Power is the people. Not
Everything depends on you.

✤

Ma Maponya looks up. She has just finished
Washing and wiping the fouled
Cement steps round the front
Of this building. She seems to discover
No horror in the bucket, no dead mirror
Of her days — merely the fact
Of one job done, another about to be
Begun. 'So will
Freedom be,' I say aloud, squatting
On the top wet step. But she
Chuckles and shakes her head.

'You!' she warns, wagging one finger. 'You!
Hamba wena! Waste of time. You talk too much.'

Kiss Me Quick

My older brother used to hoard them.
'Pussy,' he always explained, tasting the word
With a funny smile. 'Pussy pages.'
Across the centrefold
Some arch young model knelt,
Bold breasts naked,
Sizing me up.
Between her thighs,
A dainty
Tinsel
Star,
And on her face,
A pout.
To top
It all,
She dangled a toy
Revolver,
Her forefinger just
Squeezing its trigger.
'Pussy, punk!' my brother told me. 'Now, get out.'

I had to obey. I even forgot. Until
Today, sweating and sick
And forty, flipping through *Time* magazine
In the doctor's cold white waiting room
And terribly afraid of death,
I found this young
Filippino guerilla, black
Hair spilling loose
About her face, bare elbows

Braced in leopard crawl,
Breasts just beginning
But neatly suppressed
By the cut of the uniform,
Sweet face hard and
Pure
And exact, AK
Aimed at me
Pointblank:

          And
'Yes!' I whispered. 'Yes,
Kill me quick.'

Deela Khan

Liquid Borders

Love

Love moves slowly
like a hot, bright, slithering,
snake in me
It burns me inside-out
It flips me upside-down
Like an airborne flap-jack
making a crash landing
boom into the hot frying pan I hop
Like love's heavenly feeling that
makes me go through hell

And how I survive these fiery escapades
I don't know
And though I get lashed by love
ever so often
Love reigns supreme
What a scream!

And lifting me high in its death-beak
Love makes me pine and hurt and
whine and squirm
Love
reduces me to
a ruddy WORM!

Guardian of God's Great Creatures
For the English Department, BUSH

They've become kind of strange, those
erstwhile friends of hers.   Now   that
the Raj, has decorated wonder-woman with a
laurel crown,   she has become disarmingly
profound. She rests her success on
five unending days of complete
deprivation   that birthed her
mass-produced masterpieces which turned
institutional holy cows on their heads.
> I hear seventh-hand   that their
> sacred work glowed in typographical
> splendour — that its surface resplendence
> suggested worship, itself. Such work,
> all agreed, would be defiled
> were it to be fingered....
> were it to be scrutinized. So
> the work rests within its magic while
> the virtuosos conserve their facades.

Hung low for all to see:

EIGHT BRAND NEW PRIESTS UNLEASHED

to preach the Word
in borrowed light.

Photographs & Memories
For my father (22.11.1910 - 22.2.1976)

As I watch your face locked in the picture-frame
Baba, I know tonight   your Yumpy,
first-born, girl-child who cried for the moon,
made you show her the stars,
who adored donkeys & horses & flowers,
sat on your lap   almost a grown woman
has to decide   what a woman's got to do.

    Your child has inherited your eternal
    depth for compassion love for words   ear for melody.
    Composer of lyrics

                self-made philosopher
          singer   poet
             father-friend.
    Your tunes still echo in the core of me.
You lived through two wars, suffered the
battle-scars of living — but through it all
somehow you grew to transcend the
business of being, itself.
In your latter years, with fast-failing health
you still found time to heal
the ailing and barren and disturbed.
    I still don't know why I warred with you
    till the end till the very end.
You left me no time to spill tears,
    count the years laid waste by wars:
    all that destruction
    all those uncalled for tirades.
    The fact that I loved you was   bombed away.

You were Begy's Baba   when you left
your beloved last-born   at ten.   You
made her the bearer of a legacy
as large as life.   But your spirit must
rejoice as you see her grown into the
strong woman-magician   you wanted her to be.
 Your baby has rescued me from waste
 far more times than
 I'd care to recount.
I could not look at your dead face
the face I covered with kisses
 chubby arms and fingers playfully
 thrown around your neck
 your child.

It has taken me fourteen long years to re-live you
to try to decipher the hieroglyphs
drawn on the wall behind your eyes.
 You, shaman, you make me uncover
 your message of life
 healing
 creation:
I will live more true to life
I will remember all I can
I will grow
I will create:
Art will sprout from my fingers and
rush to the rescue of dying things and
dying dreams.

'.................?'

Fellow walker
You talked about the past we had to redeem:
sparks of memory that had to be caught and bottled
to stop them from going irretrievably —
She walked through the doorway of her historical present
as shrinks, occupational therapists, nurses with
needles of pain   lined the avenue-table.
Oral and ward round burst their liquid borders.
She sat stunned on the fire-stool as
dragons clothed in the images of her friends
chipped at the stone of her sanity.
His majesty the Father burned bright
at the head of the alter.
His archangel presided over the rites with his trident.
   She who rides the sea
     paints the flowers
       mends the animals and trees
had to be scanned   had to be killed.
They tried
to strip her of every grain of worth
to arrow her darkness
to reveal the light at her core
to sink into her shawls of shadow
to unleash the primal howl from the
canyons of her being
   The glare was blinding
   the voices droned endlessly on
   to deafen
      to mute
        to mutilate.

They crucified her to fertilize a
patch of weeds to decorate the
sinking halls of learning.
The walker who once deluded herself into
finding the lost road
now builds the highway
future generations will walk.

Man of Letters
In memoriam Richard Rive

Man of Letters
Why've you sung your
Life's song before noon?
You laughingly swore you'd
Sing again before dusk! Now — your
Death's Written Black, as papers display the
Mindless brutality
Endemic in our time.

You fleshed the razed tenements with
Bustle and tune in your ends to
Chronicle the Lives who struggled
Lived and loved, in your
Living Ghost-town

Spinner of yarns and dreams, it's the
Hurting void that wounds. Yet your
Voice and effervescence drum on.

That you were hacked down in
Ghetto-terror. It's this that
Knifes the Gut.

Cocktail Party Effect

My ears pricked as his name slithered
through the drone of cafeteria chatter.
'He's a walking cock....'
she said, convinced.
'I hurled him right out of my life but
as always, he landed on his feet
unscathed.'
He was my friend.
Colliding with hurt, I was forced to
admit that the tale was true.
Tears ran their paths as she sat there
alone. Does she
give him up?
He, one of the few who
peopled her life?
I walked away
hardened,
upright and strong.
It's to life that
I belong.
No man
will shatter my song!

Words Are Cheap

She'd given him all that woman could, maybe
more than a woman would or should.
Then, was ever a flaring flame so recklessly blasted,
or a farewell as nonchalant as this?
'I will give you a shout,' he muttered abruptly,
(after the bruising barbs had stung).
Then placed the receiver, his voice faded out.

Long conversations talked through and
called in his own head.
There are no telegraph poles and
no phones in the
countries of the head.

What's she left with, some may ask:
His face, far too memorable for lamentation,
yet grown so fast to his mask;
his voice which strummed her heartstrings
now pierces her heart; and the
rude awakening, that
wracked her dreams and
split her sleep:

WORDS ARE CHEAP!

Epigram on Lovers

Blessed be the blind sulphurous lovers who forge
iron-linked bonds in hope that Love's tattered rope would
ferry them across Life's treacherous waterfalls.

Busride to Campus

Like a slow-moving tide
lethargy sweeps me off balance.
I'm swamped in bogs of inertia.
My mind rustles its desiccated leaves,
I feel so dead my bones squeak.

The bus broils with unwelcome sun
which lulls me drowsy.
Stale tobacco-stink
smoke & odours
smoke my tenderised brain.
I reel and rock all the bumpy Bellville way.

Half-alive in the first period
I listen   I partake   I attend
          I switch off.
I come back to find I'm lost.

The mind desperately fights the descending fog
but capitulates to fragmentation.
The lecture becomes a distant rumble,
the lecturer a blurred voice in the Bush,
the student a trapped fly in a matchbox.

Impotence in the Face of Death

Let love go to the dogs.
I war with my warring spirit.
Let people sink in excreta.
Madness flakes my reason.
Death hounds and hollows and clogs.

I'm brittle, I crack
I creek, I scratch.
Snapped is reason's tensile stretch.

Animation ebbs as life drips through her veins.
Her slurred words drop, stuck and
ricochet as they wrench
my impotent gaze.

I watch her,
a pallid ebbing thing —
shrinking, creeping,
flickering
till death trips her light.

Mediaeval Smokescreen

Sing us a ballad Julia
you wring the strings of hearts.
When nature's all a-burgeoning
love lies frozen fast.

We hear the gun-groans splutter
as children burst their hearts....
brain and bone-blown thistles....
as the seeds of pain are ground.

Our air is dank with spirits
of lost bodies
in crude graves. No priests
no kin...no service....
no lives nor souls to save.

Your voice's so soothing Julia....
but your lyric's far removed.
It's so nice to savour innocence....
it's so pretty and so unreal.

Change your tune my lovely Julia....
Splash your lines with fire of the age.
Nourish your song with the
starvation of body and soul....
Fit it with killermachines, and
blow it with blighted love, and
Nature's rust and the psychopath's lust....
And your ballad will lift our souls.

The world turns swaddled in its womb of blood
as blood kills and sluices and floods and
clots and rots with the bloodlines of the ages.

Sing on, your tune is catchy
it wends its way to the head.
Blaze on, your song is scorching
it oils the fires of pain.

Barbed Words

Do my words work?
And if they do, do they tell true,
do they begin to bare reality?

> Do they hold the
> > flagrant flames of our
> > > searing present?

Do they singe
> the furrowed pain
> > tiered with terror
> etched in the prisoner's pallor;
> > the anguish wracking the hours
> of the bomb-blown child's mother
> watching harried hopes miscarried
> as dreams fall, break and
> dissipate into lethargy;
> > the human torches
> > > and bullet-slashed brains
> > and the swooping price of life

as inflation soars;
and the rifts and fissures that split our thought;
and a hint of spectral hope for a better land,
a better life,
a better world,
a better universe:
do they singe home?

Home, that offers my so overworked
words, some rest.

Monday Morning Observation

For my tutorial group

It's such a pleasure to watch
the sweet honey-dears
in my tut.

They shuffle in all a-flutter
flock into chairs all
animatedly a-twitter
as they relate the
glamour and the glitter
of the weekend
just flown past.

The sprightly sparrows settle down
when sparkling ivory at its preened best
wings in. The fragrance of the
herb garden below, wafts in
through the window and lifts

the fog from clogged senses.
An unholy silence descends
as they bend their faces
intently savouring her melodious cooing.

The dove praises her flock of sparrows'
creative craftmanship. They squawk
with ecstasy as they bathe
in the geysers of her esteem.

Forty lusty minutes of uninterrupted melody sustained.

Notes to synchronise
with the vibrations of impoverished souls.

Self-censorship

It has long been legit for poets to
pepper poetry with 'swear words'. Our
vital model, Serote, doesn't squirm to
write: 'What's in Black Shit?' but my
dropping the bombshell, 'SHIT', causes
an uproar in B-Four.

The woman activist hurls meeting jargon:
'That student must be called to order
she will not take the liberty to abuse
language here!'

Lecture Hall etiquette must be adhered to
at all times
at all costs.

Does the poet bow to the prattling banal
women of her befogged third-year class,
to the slack impotent men of her final-
year class? Does she rattle and break
in the wake of their
groundless onslaughts?

If constructs are relative,
if dogma is relative,
if perception is
relative, the poet
is insulated by her licence!

Her self-righteously arrogant class-
mates dissipate into a scolding mob
of rabble-rousers.

Black Monday

Death swept through our roads in lorry-loads.
The shots of shame skulked in crates
and waited...
they waited.

Brakes screeched, the air stifled
and smothered,
Gun shots, guts wrenched, hearts leaped
and Death's bullets blasted
their fragile bodies....

Striding through terror and tumult
through storms of tears with wracked souls
people were wailing:
no-no-no
they're killing our kids
a sobbing mother
oh God where's my child
a tortured teacher
can the dead one be Michael
he's missing...might be dead.

And our streets bear testimony to the scourge:
streets dappled and blazing with coagulated patches of
life's stream.

Tears cannot wash away the sorrow,
sorrow cannot strip the scars:
scars that will scathe and scorch
record the time!

The struggle-strangled seedling
against all odds
will thrust its head
towards the sun.

Trojan Horse: Athlone, 15 October 1985.

Psychotherapy
For JS

Four o'clock
Ready to face my session of shocks
Your office
Two chairs facing each other
Enveloped in a haze of barrenness,
sterility, desolation and frugality
You and I
You sit facing me
A pair of soft hazel eyes peering into me,
watching imperturbably   missing nothing.
Adorable vulture, nothing escapes your gaze:
I bite my nails, you see it. I blink my eyes,
you catch it. I writhe in pain, you perceive
it. I tell you my life —
You say nothing.
I become uneasy, my flesh starts to creep
supernatural notions mute my mind
Are you a woman or a ghost or a
camera photographing my life?
You are a camera

Your shutter clicks on all those
irretrievable moments of transience.
You catch me off guard   You heighten
my flaring tongues of anger   You capture
my mannerisms, my expressions, You net
naked me exposed — Inflamed,
cringing with indignation and abhorrence
I shrink, shrink!
You entrap my fleet, furtive glances when
my eyes flirt with yours. A fragile balance
of space and time is caught forever and locked
in your mind. Yet, your're so indifferent.
Please don't act concerned.
I appreciate you most when you don't even
try to clothe your face with caring looks.
Maybe, I'm too hard on you. You're still so
young, so limited, you've not been around too
long. You're still developing emotionally,
groping dangerously, fighting to find your feet
while your client's desperately
pursuing her elusive
identity.

Numinous Moments
For SV

Wandering through streams and rivers of faces
I floated between gaps of human forms
My blurred vision cleared for a face
       your face

The brush of your body...
the faint touch of your hand...and
my ears attuned to the nuances and inflexions
of a musical familiar voice
       your voice
Like violins abound
how I savoured the sound

Your fingers led me across Adderley Street in a daze
Your human touch set glowing my frozen blood
with gushing warmth
And it was so good to hear you talk
and to have you care
and to know this business called living
is not nearly so bland and bare

So pass on such doses of caring
in attempt to get a world
devoid of sharing
to care
if it dares

Matthew Krouse

Currents of Flesh

When You Have Killed My Mother

Boykie — when you have killed my mother
And bruised my sister and before you kneel in the street
To rub the sticks that make fire
Rest on my bed and see my torn ceiling, the bloody hole
The sweating sky. Rest on my bed and pat my dog.
My pets will not feed on you if you have fed on them.
You can eat my dog. But don't eat my toy trainset
Or my inflatable survival kit or my scout's honour.

I know that you fathered the plants
You plaited the curtain tassel and tickled my walls
With a feather duster. Lie on my bed now
And see our ceiling torn into a bloody gaping cunt
Sweating from the sky. If you roll over
I will scratch the landscape of your back
My fingers will undo that battlefield
While you rape my telephone. Don't eat my sweets now
Rather slot our record collection into my fat piggy-bank
Into a sack on your back clanging with porcelains and
The frozen french loaf. I have lots of cotton wool
We can dress you up as Father Christmas and glitter
Your bronze eye
Then we can paint your toenails for the carnival
And feast. And I will tattoo an image
Of the forgiving Madonna behind your terrified ear.

There will be no conclusion to my giving
Because I have so much there will be
No conclusion to your taking because
You will see so many fatty deposits
And thick-walled hearts.

There on my ground I will lie and tear my clothes
Don sack cloth and sacrifice a chicken.
There on your ground you will tear off your clothes
Don beads and sacrifice a goat. The mud
Will melt with the blood and we will lift
Our enamel mugs to the sky showing our ancestors
This new porridge and the recipe
In defiance of hell.

And when we have built a wall between ourselves
And the setting sun we will look to the
Lampshade made of the hide of my dad
And we will gently turn the switch
To pray for eternal light. And I will say
I did nothing I just watched history
And you will say you did nothing
You just watched history
And poetry will be reborn.

The storms will make rushing rivers and the rushing rivers
Will make electricity and from the pitiful ground
Will grow the trees that made this transparent paper
Showing me yesterday's words
Through its delicate veins.

Blue Lips

In this instance they kissed. He let go his kite and lost it.

In this instance they kissed he let go and lost it and she said:
You have blue lips.
Those are excuses he said and she said:
You have blue lips.
Excuses. There are women with coffee stains
and sweat around their necks. They wait for the rain
on hotter days. There is Benoni and there is Germiston
and there is Fox Street and they walked down all three
to see his mother. His brother was wet. His brother was
consummated by the stormy season, circumcised
by a couple of tramps and jealous of him. She liked him
she said: You have blue lips.
Everyone heard and everyone saw the school blazer
of the younger brother fall from his shoulders
before they fucked.
There was social trauma. The house was full. Full of shame.

That two brothers fucked one woman that one woman
had fucked two brothers. That a woman could.
I asked her she said yes. She said to me:
You have blue lips.

I looked in my mirror. My lips were round.
She had said they were blue.
I stood in the park in Lambton Germiston. I fiddled.
There was a shoal of orphans playing on a swing.
There was a fat matron
hiding behind an embroidered smock.

She came nearer and spoke. She said and she spoke
and she said and she spoke and she carried a broken twig
and she said:
You have blue lips.
I looked in the mirror. My lips were round.

In retrospect I wonder if all women
tell men these things. I ask my friends. I see
my lips in my mirror. They are round.
When last I saw a woman I asked her.
Tell me about the blue lips.
She said:
They are dead.

The Rest is History

I
The Catholics pray
that someday the whole world will be Catholic.

My every thought turns to the altar
upon which you will be placed with your
nervous lip between your very nervous itchy teeth
through the cheap cosmetic body paint
you will sweat.
Like the trace elements of thunder
you will sweat.

Precious stones precious stones
they will find in your kidneys
with emerald clots on your brain
and the purest water on your knee.
And I will lift you from the mob

And I will take you to a place
where television
is like fruit on a tree.
And that is only half as happy
as you will be with me.

I CONSIDER THESE WORDS THE ONLY
BARGAINING POINT I HAVE.

The strongest boat is pulled by the strongest wave
the strongest wave floats on a current of flesh.
The flags are the pimples of desire
in those family sagas on television
where lounges stare at lounges
and divorcees stare at divorcees
and mistakes stare at mistakes
in the bathroom and in town
and in the butchery
and in the car
and on holiday
and the ghastly list of social irregularities continues.

Sin — ladies and gentlemen — and I mean your sins
are in your backyards ladies and gentlemen.
It is in the frightened moments you spend alone
every day
when the mirror cannot lie
to you
about yourself
about your former self
and about the future you will not know
even when you get there.
I am also sorry that the suburbs
we so immaculately designed
for ourselves are not working.

One bad party leads to another
and while standards are dropping
there is sometimes no time
to ask the crucial questions
about that line from your nose to your mouth
that scoops out your cheek with each passing day
that curbs the smile of your lip
that makes it impossible to emigrate
that sees household pets come and go
that sees so many competitions on so many boxes
in so many newspapers on so many radio stations
through so many pretty lips on such pretty paper.
Competitions. I hate competitions
because competitions draw such thick lines
between winners and losers.

Your dark eyes are growing confused
and your regiment of ideas
is going with your thousand loves
on a barge down the Nile. And now
you turn to the revolution
and you ask it for an overcoat
for a rainy day.

II

I notice that even the skin of the cactus
stretches tightly around the skeleton of its form.
But the light blue carcasses
that judge us of our treason
the flaking eyes that are our eyes
before the works of ages are bowing in disgust.
Everyone is feverish with the plague.
Everyone has been taught the strictest lesson in hate.
Yet the carrion dishes the diseased into their graves.

We are the unfortunate cultivated
We are the investment investigated
We are unemployed and mismanaged
We have a christian education.

ONCE WE WERE RUNNING AT A PROFIT
BUT NOW WE ARE RUNNING AT A LOSS.

This is how time is built
in its hot and bothered space
with its slow honest pace.

Such is the perfect produce of earth
that some judge others by their shoes.
These are the ones who do the walking,
while those who are kneeling judge others
by the wooden warts on their knees.

One written statement follows another
until thoughts become newspapers and novels
and people are needed to sell them.
This is the genius of the modern world
that pays for its love
in figures that would shock the president.

Cast an eye over your territory
see the legs of your chairs
among your licences for dogs
and empty lunchboxes.
See every appliance of yours
just slow down and die.

THIS IS THE WAY OF THE EARTH
WHEN IT TURNS TO LOOK AT ITSELF
WHEN IT WALKS ITS AMBITIONS IN A FULL CIRCLE
AND DROWNS ITSELF
IN THE HOLE THAT IT HAS BURNT IN THE SOIL.

III
My thoughts of you are only the entrance
to an entire civilization of thinking.
It's only that my car will not start
on our first night out.
It's only my cheap silly lighter
that will not burn
enough to ignite the cigarette
between those solid lips
that shut me out.

These are the nights I am speaking of
when the tenants in the crowded stone monuments
commemorate their evictions in a festival of rain
where every kitten born to every smiling virgin
is part of the same tragic suction
on the largest breast we know.

WORDS ARE USELESS
WHEN THE FLOORBOARDS ARE SHIVERING
AH WELL THANK GOD
THE NEWSPAPERS ARE ON TIME.

We are gluttons and our strange fetish for tea and coffee
has taught us to overcome our afternoon fears.
We can play tennis and we can dance well
we can play our pretty musical instruments
we can write easy letters
we can converse politely
we are frightening and colonial
we are called educated.

We resemble the two colours of wine
that can be drunk with fish
with chicken or blood red meat
with the insides of the stomach
becoming a little pinker
becoming a little redder
becoming a little blacker
and smoother and browner
with all of that money
for that fancy french name
going down the toilet bowl
along with the dreams.

There are two kinds of food
good food and bad food
and bad food walks in a thin disguise
it lingers like love in a restaurant
and hammers on the back door for a job.

The moral life is the perfect judgement
of space from the bed to the kitchen
and from the carport outwards
until the only expulsion
is an even plateaux of energy
without deviation from what is necessary
and just within a given second.

The only commitment is a commitment to peace
the rest is termed political which means
that the movement is only

a strategic reorganisation of people
into one mighty fat fist.

And yet
we are afraid to change

not in our brand of marriage
and not in our make of car

we cannot let go of our adult problems
in this baby country

where we are scared to scratch our knees
scared of the scars and burns of grass

and the first flames
of the stoves.

Weep women weep.

A woman is a planet.

And the rest is history.

Yellow Ale

Half of my hearing has been stolen
It is the half that hears a cry
And feels sympathy.
Half of my face is missing.
It is the half that was unwrinkled

At school.
Some of my reasons are running truant.
Reasons I never got from
Presidents, mayors, generals or cops.

It's as if life were a photograph
Made merely of paper, plastic and light.
You, in fatigues. Dogtag glowing.
Tanks made of second hand cars
Bent rifles, burning rubber
Cushions made of sand
Bombs filled with sulphur
Sleep that is interrupted
Urinating on command
Killing by demand.

So don't give me your contribution
To science or law or art
Because I might start to show you
How things fall apart.
How things fall apart.

And now, young soldier
You might as well bath with me in ale
Before your stature grows frail
And your complexion grows pale
You might as well bath with me
In this yellow ale.

We had better share this garden
Before our fathers blow it up.

Come Taxi

Let us steer away
To where the clubbing cannot dent your only face,
This is no place.

We'll make an exchange. My torn trousers
For your golden shirt, my problem will be the sun
And your problem can be the moon. This is home.
Welcome home. Sorry, home is still a colonel's dick
Whose sultry ways were built by prisoners.
Are we allowed in this room?
Is this room ours now, may we decorate it?
Can we hang your dad's picture in it?
Are we allowed to hate your father in this marriage?
I have declared myself too often.

Please could you join our conversation club.
We like to talk. We compare ourselves to each other
And then we rate and then we test
And we compare and we rate and we test.
It's mere distraction and we never get past the headlines.
Can we come in now?
I want to fuck your teacup
And you can rest my barstool against your leg.
This is two thirds but I want one hundred percent.

Come taxi. I am going. And you must take me away.
I am flexible but the war is not.
Right now I'm going to Sun City for a fuck.

Oh boy. Every morning I have to get up
to declare:
I am alone.

My Secret

Gee God I'm so lonely here without my dead friends
Lonely and unhappy as the years roll on
It stops mattering. Tell me, what chance is there
That we might scan the ages without finding
Our own mistakes. The boy broke down.
Is he a car and will we fix him? There's salt
In my eyes.
Oh hatred has sent his ambassador to call.
I light my candles and I shake out my shoes
And I find you in the dust under my foot
And I find you in the dirt in the corner of my room
And they have gone. They have gone to remind us
Who they are. Not who they were.
And when we find them
Feeding like only the dead can, on our mistakes
Then what hope is there that we will correct them?
I would tell you. But it's a secret.

Cinema of Good Hope

There can be no playing in the rain
if there is no rain
There can be no racing through the storm
if there is no storm
And if your customs of your clan
amount to nothing and rubbish
Then you had better find other customs in another clan.

Death will not disfigure you unless you are dead.
And telephones will not ring if there is no phone.

If the gun fires then use all the rounds
And don't stop until everyone is dead.
Kill sunshine if the trends are against friends.
Kill the telephone, and when the lines are down
Cook spaghetti in blood. Join the parade!

Here comes Consolation. But she can only remind.
Here comes Forgiveness. But she can only forgive.
There goes the clock. But it will never turn back.
Famous has come and Famous has gone
Even archaeology cannot trace her whereabouts
Without offering only here a broken pot
and there a soggy frieze.

Look how everybody is divided
Crying in one voice. That's unity for you!
This terrible Good is dancing with that beautiful Evil.
While we are here on our Mountain of Love.
What should we wear as they bury this idea?
A flag?

Where this land ends there is a cross and then a drop.
Where this land ends there is nothing, not even sea.
So here is my message of hope: Enjoy!
Because you are going nowhere. You're staying home.

Time will take care of you too, my lovely
And then we will love, when we are both ugly.

Oh shit. Shit. Shit. I have eaten.
But here is some hope: Go to the cinema
Learn everything there is.
And relish the darkness.

Negotiating

I feel that your anus is the true and only monument
To perfection on God's earth. Pristine and eurocentric,
Oh definitely more so than the observed dates
Of great sacrifices and suicides.
I am therefore plotting the necessary route to heaven
A place where all will vote and none will suffer.
Your opening is charming my every decision
For when I write these poems
I am forced to negotiate
With an anus.

I am negotiating with an anus.
There is an element of mistrust when canvassing for votes
A desperate need to justify the killing
Dinner party conversation becomes a scream
And there is an air of capture
The exploitation is far from over
When negotiating with an anus.

The reason there are sickly bodies
Is because there are sickly minds.
Devastation that will never be forgotten.
Someday we will have said goodbye to hatred
But for now there is still so much to do
The lounge has so many ornaments that need breaking
Youth, so many charms for the taking.
I'm telling you this
Because inside you are warm
There is a lovely natural calm
About your anus.

Torture

And so the torturer begins his work long before dawn
Hours and hours into your precious sleep
He is sharpening his blades
And charging the electric prong and dipping the hood
Into ice cold water
While you are asleep mother and father
And you turn twice to snore
And to wheeze while the torturer
Sharpens his blades.

So don't bother to get up in the morning
After a night on the frozen floor
Unless you are called for by five men in raincoats
With thick small town accents
With no eyes set in vomiting pools
Just keep breathing
And don't bother to get up in the morning
When your lip and your spine
Are aching and sore.

Oh yes there are public holidays
If you want to see the shores and the lakes
And while you are relaxing in that beauty
Just think of the meat and then taste the gravy
And pack the boot
And phone the police around mid-morning
To thank them for the order
To thank them for the peace
And to thank them for the torturer
Who began his work long before dawn.

Frontline State

What do the neighbours think of us
When we borrow their lawnmower
Without returning it?
What do the neighbours think
When we tear down the fence between our gardens
And we play our games, ripping up their lawn?
What do they think of us
When we invade their kitchen
And we eat their food?

What do the neighbours' children think of us
When we forbid our children from playing with them?
What do our neighbours think
When we send our children over to attack their children
Leaving them without arms or legs?

Our children ask no questions
Because we cut out their tongues.

But what do our neighbours think of us
When we gossip about them
To our friends?
Are we the kind of neighbours
That we would like to have?

Why should we even give a damn.
If our neighbours complain about us
We'll just kill them!

Banish the Serpent

Hammer on the doors of the unhappy people
And tell them there is reason to celebrate
The old ways must be killed now. Gone
Are the punishments if we will them away.
Look at the dying leadership of tattered old men
Keeping their heads together between bricks.
Their talk of a new dispensation is covering
Our old wounds.
These cranky rotting white lions are mangy.
These braindead old elephants with sore tusks.
These stupid geriatric politicians must get off
The train now. Home was two stops back
Where the sad corpses of Hottentots still take revenge
On the bones of ancient slavekeepers who taught
The rhinos of today their evil perverted legislative tricks.
Parliament is a brothel. Government Avenue is a sewer.
There is only one reality. Banish the serpent.

Hammer on the doors of everyone you know.
Fling the ones of understanding asunder.
Only humans shall make law. Animals will be harnessed.
Animals will never bite again.
Girls will go about their labour
And boys will go about their labour.
No one will be old then.
Used will again be useful.
Colour will again be colourful.
Trust will be reborn.
And hard work will continue
To undo the shameful stitches
Joining the ugly wounds of time.

Oh Lachrymose

Oh lachrymose, how the tears ran down her face
On the day her lover said goodbye.
She left him clutching his triumphant new girlfriend
Who ran a disco in a hotel where everyone would go.
(Her panties, his jockies playing on the floor.)

I went to the bar
To swap some information on the coming revolution
But I found it empty except for the barman
And the old lady wearing sideburns who keeps the door.

Oh lachrymose, how she wandered from shop to shop
Once her precious womb had been stabbed and cut.
She tried to phone her best friend.
At the Post Office she cried in the queue
Remembering his salmon skin in her mouth.

I rolled a cigarette at the Wimpy cafe
Then popped into the indoor pool for a swim.
In the locker room I folded my trousers neatly
Fearing for the safety of my banking card and money.

Oh lachrymose, she even went past the people's clinic
To fetch her contraceptive pill.
As she swallowed it she cherished the lump in her throat
Forgetting for a moment how children are born
And that loneliness can be indestructible.

I went past the chemist
To buy some condoms in a fancy sunset pack.
I went back to the bar then to chat up my buddy
But it had closed so I chucked the rubbers in the bin.

Oh lachrymose, she really had nowhere to go
And when she found a room the roof was leaking.
So she patched up the hole then sat on her finger
To rediscover her desire for lasting pleasure.
That's how she began to practise pleasure, real
                    and everlasting.

Last time I saw her she was still practising pleasure
She was wearing a bold and new funny face
So I asked her if she was living only for her finger
But she just smiled then laughed and laughed.

(At last she was discovering
The innermost secret of her funky soul.)

Art

When the last kid in town turns to go
and looks at his uptight parents
who will never ever know.
He throws a stone into the water
and puts a bull-ring through his nose
he'll wear a fishook through his foreskin
while the gang sprays a synagogue.
No, there are no conflicts greater
than the conflicts of the heart

the only true salvation
is in the state of the art.
I'd like to sum up with guerilla warfare
I'd like to drive you to despair
but I'll throw away this jargon
to say it in terms that are there:
There are no conflicts greater
than the conflicts of the heart.
The only true salvation
is in the state of art.

Rushdy Siers

Horse Milk and Other Poems

I Literate

When I could not write
they knew my name better than I
when I could not read
they knew my life better than I;
where I came from
where I should go
what I should do
then I decided to carve an 'A'
in the very ground where before I could only
leave the print of my sole
I battled to shape the big buttocked 'B'
in the ever changing clouds which hid a world I so
much wanted to see
I struggled to link letters to the simply curved 'C'
in the many winding tunnels of my illiterate dreams
longing for that moment
in the face of sympathetic eyes
when I can discard that faceless 'X'
whose ghost haunts my life between the
endless dotted lines
to declare in bold hard determined strokes
the letters, the words, the thoughts, the works
buried in my name
Ndim Lo!

Te Danke aan Kenilworth

I
Daar is 'n kans
moenie jou kaartjie gee aan die wind
die eerste been is gewen
die tweede been is in
die derde onrustig as die perde voor die wegspringstalle
spring
daar is 'n kans

II
Daar is 'n kans
jou kaartjie nou 'n skoenlapper wat dwaal in jou maag
die derde been het geslaag
die vierde nou pas net-net met 'n neus oor die lyn geskraap
die vyfde vol angs wat 'n lange half uur nou nog vertraag
daar is 'n kans

III
Daar is 'n kans
bid aan god Equus al is dit dom
die vyfde been het huis toe gekom
die tote dit paper as hul jou wen opsom
die SESDE, die laaste, die hekke spring, die perde in volle
vaart — kom
daar is 'n kans

IV
Daar is 'n kans
jou oë dop om jou kaartjie geskeer
jou laaste been is deur 'n donkie probeer
Ag dis all right die een was vir meer as perde voer
maar kom gerus vanaand terug en sit tog en hoor
daar is 'n kans

V
Daar is 'n kans
tussen die mens se verlore kaartjies, verdwaalde siele en
gebroke drome
die ironie ou maat die ironie
luister nou na die rumoer
daai oulike ou klein paddas is oproerig
daar is 'n kans

VI
Daar is 'n kans
die gesondste fynbos in die kaap te kry
gerus in 'n paar gekampte hektar te wy
more kan ons altyd vir jou 'n ou beentjie opfix
maar sekerlik in die lewe is daar...
wat meer as 'n outside kans moes kry en dit nogal in
PICK SIX

'n Gat in die Dak

Daar's 'n gat in die dak —
vat 'n loer
die jol gaan nog voort
dis blind my broer
o'se priorities is oneway opgescrew

Daar's 'n gat in die dak, my broer
die fokken CFC's is in oproer

'Ow, watter mobsters is die nou weer boeta Joe?

Naai nie mobsters nie ou
Dis die goeters wat hulle in die aerosol blikkies goei
en 'n klompie ander goeters soos die gas in die fridges,
check daai is die CFC's, en nou is die dak aan die lek
Daar's 'n gat in die dak my broer

'Watse dak is die boete Joe?

Die blou my broer, die grote blou, check
dis die atmosphere wat os protect
van al die laser beams wat van die son af straal
en al die ander mal ninjas wat in outer space rond dwaal

'Ow, what kind, boeta Joe, met diese human race?
Ja-nee, Ja-nee nou raak jy wys

Daar's 'n gat in die dak —
vat 'n loer
die jol gaan nog voort
dis blind my broer
o'se priorities is oneway opgescrew

Growth

On a morning
my daughter then barely five and I
walked in that little pine wood
on the slopes of Signal Hill
above the noon gun lazing in the truce of Sunday
peace
while the city pigeons cooed relief
no frenzied noon day flight today — declared
with spongy gait we ambled atop years of soft
leafy compost
springing....

On that morning
in the little pine wood — there
a rotting rodent corpse
we gaped in awe at the writhing maggots inside
rippling life like rhythms along the tattered flank
of the dead remains
the maggots weaving in the way of all flesh
and in and out among themselves
feasting....

On that morning
coming out of the little pine wood
on the gravel path — there
a dehydrated coke tin
littering....
in disgust I kicked it
clanking empty screams
skidding over stone and into a ditch
a lone tear dropped from its eye
crying....

On that morning
along that gravel path — there
just as the noon gun was supposed to boom
a dead pigeon in the way
its wings spread
frozen, motionless
lying....

On that afternoon
there — my daughter begged
to take all these treasures home with her
but I advised amidst complaints
but as her sights were already set
to catch up with the people
speckled in the distance ahead
like her fickle years
and much to my relief
she jettisoned her new found treasures
for the ambitious goal ahead
she tugged me from my dilemma along with her
running....

On that afternoon
if we had taken the treasures found along our
walk
on coming home,
what could I have said?

Here is a dead rat
we have brought it home for you to see.

Behold! here is a dead rat
the living testimony of the death of the animal —

in us
we have brought it home for you to see —
see!

Behold! Here is the dehydrated coke tin
a weeping product of that disposable culture
we kicked aside on our walk along the man
made path
we have brought it home for you to see —
see!

Behold! here is a dead bird
with wings spread wide —
its flight frozen in time
as are the booming of the guns
of yesterday's war, yesterday's struggle
we have brought it home for you to see —
see!

But
On that afternoon
as it were
impatient youth led me from that alien forest
where we took our very first spring-like steps
to gallop along that endless quest after our
humanity
speckled in the distance
a worthy goal growing bigger and stronger
as we draw ever, ever closer
towards the growing concept of our being —
human.

Sets of Two and their Silence

Today children our lesson will be about sets....
Kanalla cheacher nie vandagie.

Does every body know what a set is?
Yaa, a snytjie brood en a snytjie brood maak a sanwich.

Good, please pay attention and don't look so sleepy!
Ek slaap tot ek dai klokkie hoor — kostyd!

Many things and any number of things can make a set....
Ek wonne wat gan op 'ie brood wies?

For example, a tea set and a cutlery set....
Nou moet jy nogal van kosgoed praat.

Can anyone give me an example of a set? quickly....
Set and ready to go, as ek dai klokkie hoor.

Class what is wrong?
Niks verkeet 'ie net honger.

Can nobody give me an example of a set?
Cheacher lat ek net slaap tot netnou.

Children you must pay attention!
Ya a snytjie brood en a snytjie brood maak a sanwich.

And why this silence?
Jy's fokken doef as jy nie my maag kan hoor nie!

Horse Milk

Woman child
the things I sometimes recall
like, trying to pick flowers from a linoleum floor,
crying for grandpa going away on a train journey,
drinking horse milk from the blacksmith's jug.
I see his blackened nails.
I see my father's smile he says:
'See, he likes it.'
I see the blacksmith's face a rounded smile
a huge silvery moustache stained brown.
'How can you?' she asks.
'You were only one or two,
you are an impossible child,'
my mama says.
Could you love an impossible child?

A Minor Poet

Woman child
I say softly
I say tenderly,
while playing with the sound,
caressing the concept of your being
I beg —
do you know me?

If you were to look for me among
the great men of our times —
you will not see me

but if you were to walk against the great tides,
the multitudes of people
walking the daily routes in pursuit of simple life
you may in that vast ocean see me

If you were to look for my verse
in the great anthologies of my time
you will not find it
but if you were to browse the tattered pages
of life where the English is peculiar
yet the language of our lives rich and warm
you will chance across my humble verse

I stand proud
in the ranks of the great multitude of minor poets
waiting the opportunity to open
my soul, my mind, my life
for you and you to see
and feel

If this is what you want
I will share my confusions, my passions, my fears,
my knowings and not knowings
with you freely and honestly
I will take you as you are
and I will give you much, much love....

Ansar

To the Palestinians 'living' in Ansar
R.S. 28 April 1989

Umi, Umi the soldiers are coming....
Stampeding death has callous eyes.
The smell of cheap dollar deodorants
flirts with their foul sweat of an ambitious state.
My sisters wail a history of sorrow,
their cries sent fleeing — a protest in diaspora.
The Uzi's butt brands a R1 TATTOO on my flesh
it burns like a 44 year old torture in my mind,
Mama I am afraid.

Mama, the soldiers are coming....
thundering into the streets of our lives,
waking the outrageous cries of our dead,
hammering wedges of iced fears into my heart.
Hold me Mama.
Hold me and crush this agony.
Hold me close Mama your warmth, your tears
nourish our buring desires that make
the fences 'round Sabra shiver with anger,
the fences 'round Shatila shake impatiently,
summoning ghosts and echoes from Auschwitz and Belsen
to lament with the living in Ansar.
Hold me close Mama,
for now let us arrest this fear.

Addressing the Language Question
To Wally Serote and Willy Kgositsile

I
am
a black
man
my name
Keorapetse Serote Rushdy Mangone Kgositsile
the colonial mind smiles
patronising, intolerant, superior, arrogant and prejudiced
the colonial tongue asks:
'HOW MUCH?'
                    HOW MUCH INDEED!
I
shake
my
head
in disbelief
smiling, understanding, hurt, struggle, and struggle to
forgive
it
expects
Washington, Columbus, Livingstone,
Wellington, George, Victoria
to
escape
my
mouth
to soothe

its colonial ears
Oh!
if
they
were
not
South Africa
I
would
tell
them
in
the
wisened
lyric
of
my
mother's
tongue;
fokoff!

Trek Net

die net is amper in
die lanie skop 'n bohaai op nes 'n opgewonde haan om sy harem
te herrinner dat hy nog steeds die main konyn is
so stap hy tussen die kettings van mannekrag:
'hê Sakkie, djy vry nie nou met 'n tief — trek man.
hê Balla djy lyk soos 'n fokken mannequin
wat pose virrie Sunday Times — trek jong'

hy spoek en moedig sy manskap aan
die twintig man trek en vloek teen die krag van die see
nou en dan word 'n ruskans geniet so dat die golwe weer
hulle beurt doen om die gelaaide net in te spoel
uitendelik 'dis vet! dis vet manne!' word verklaar

die net is in
Seameeue duik en skreeu soos fighter planes
op die fees van baba vis wat terug geslinger word
'n drie duim galjoen duur te land om te herstel van die skok
Zap — in sy bek en af sy keel
'n vinger lang kabeljou twyfel voor hy dyk — Zap
'n klein steenbrassie wat nog nie eens 'n kreuwel
uit die sand gesuig het nie — Zap
'n hand vol baardmannetjies — Zap, zap, zap, zap
die kolstertjies en wit stompneusies staan gun kans — Zap

die net is in
dis vet
die strandlopers en kopers
dwaal om terwyl 'n lewendige berg van haarders
'vyf vir 'n rand'
terwyl 'n half dosyn elf weggesteek word
talle galjoen is onder groen waterdig baadtjies gesmokkel
'n koper gesels met die lanie
'n paar steenbrasse gesteke tussen die twee
alles shjoep — shjap voor die wet verskyn

die net is weg
die seemeeue trommel dik, rus kip in die wind
die jol is klaar
koraal

see bamboes
rooiaas koeke
van die bodem en by die wortel uitgeruk
afgebroke penne en velle van die St Josephs
besoedel die strand
die manne gaan nou 'n doppie soetwyn drink
daar is darem ook 'n fry vir vanaand
en die lanie vreet lekker elf op 'n winters aand
met 'n berg haarders 'vyf vir 'n rand' in die agtersak
'n sware lewe diese getrekkery
swaar vir trekkers
en nog swaarde vir die see
'n noord windjie kalmeer die pyn
tot môre skyn....

Sight One

How pale will the cosmos
appear; those oceans of
expanding space, compared to
the light of day when
their eyes will be pierced by
blunted scalpel blades.
Wrenching cataracts of
arrogant visions — to see
not the soul of light,
nor the dance of an atom,
nor the movement of time,
but through a cut they will be forced to see
the sights of one sweet human life.

Sight Two

Morning came, but softly
a cautious sun
a vantage peak.
unbridled rays of majestic hues
incognito amidst the fragile veil of dark
nightmares sensing dawn flee —
releasing their romantic talons from reality

through, against
the night
the dark
the clandestine orchestra of colour advanced
a thunderous crescendo of brilliant yet subtle
note of
lights and shades shower
upon sight

Lance Nawa

South African Road

South African Road

It is quiet the way it has to be;
it's black, wide
it twists, twirls,
ascends and descends.

Tyres screech on it
Nations travel on it;
white, black, yellow, pink,
all like ants, go to and fro
east and west
west and east
north and south
south and north.

Some slow
some fast....
They all enjoy its
smooth concrete carpet....

It is a midwife,
a doctor, a labourer, a murderer,
and all.

It is a bond:
it links cities and their souls.
It is a nuisance:
it bisects mountains, overides
rivers....

It is rich: state revenues,
labourers' sweat, traffic lights, and time
bow their heads to it.

Oh, it is invaded: disunited
whites stride in the middle.
They seize control, compartmentalize
its citizens, give orders to stop,
turn left or right or to
overtake.

It is South African:
it induces people to keep
left. We are left.
What now?

Good Gone Bad

Comrades, by the time your noses
cease bobbing to your words
like idling floats,
during this meeting,
I will have written
three poems and then read them to you.
You have turned agendas into good gone bad.

Slym Hande

My ma was lakens by 'n hotel.
Sy kom altyd huis toe
met haar hande vol slym:

maar ma het 'n goeie hart
ek sal altyd uit
haar hande eet en lewe.

Hardkoppig

Here is someone as dark as
my arse talking:
'n kaffir gaan my nie sê
ek moet stayaway.
ek wil werk; ons kleurlinge
volg die prosedure
van die witmense —
die darkies is net so hardkoppig
soos hulle korrelkoppe.

Love Letters

I
The wind howled your name today
moaned it around corners
spewed it out in agony
whispered it in despair

the pull
of the wind
on your name —
did you feel it?

II
I felt it.
If I felt the pull
of the wind on my name
it was a yearn for you

If I felt the wind
spewing my name around corners
it was seeking a trace of your
timeless company

If I felt the wind moaning
it was whispering hope —
I did feel it in the wind
and in your name.

Toegedrukte Siel

Hier wag ek langs 'n posbus
met die kleur van kersfees.

Sy ronde, kenlose gesig spoeg 'n sneeu baard
rondom tralies, stoepe, bome
en 'n weeshondjies wat
op sy voorpote sit en bewe.

Sy bek, en ook dié van 'n yster Santa
is wawyd wonde waarvan geen
bloed of stemme uitgorrel.

My maag was stil, maar nou begin ek gril;
ek twyfel of jou brief ooit sal kom.

Maar ek wag. Of miskien moet ek wens
ek was 'n plat seël wat jou
toegedrukte siel sal verwarm.

Lewensomstandighede

Waar is jou sent
want ons betaal rent.

Brrrrr Bbrrrrrrr

Brrrr brrrr...nommer asseblief,
julle bly staan en praat nie!
Can I really talk to a dead line?
I've been slinging for ages for service.

Okay, gee die nommer dan.
Twee-nege-een-ses
Waar?
Hammanskraal, Temba.
Hou net aan, hoor?

...pip pip...jy is deur:
maar gooi eers dertig sent in, hoor?
En maak gou!
See, I have enough coins to slot in
the whole day.

Charred Cupid Arrows

This heart of mine has always been a hill
of solitude heaving paranoic eruptions.
Friends and foes alike are shunned
and scorched to ashes by fire-flames from veins
which are by now charred cupid arrows

Vows in a Shell

The moon, an inflated ring, intensified
our search for each other
the evening after our eyes had locked
across sparkling plates and utensils.

Chariot of time, within its circumference,
wrenches us from our doubts and reluctance
and dips us into the vast Milky-Way, and later,
onto the fine sand along littoral lines.

A shell pops out from the bitter-sweet, pure foam
and beckons me to whisper your name
into its shrine where our hearts
consummate our palpitating love.

Newspaper Boy

With a bag full of journalists
and the world on his tiny back
he dazzles between rapid-fire
traffic like a trapeze artist.

In winter, his mouth and nostrils
become exhaust pipes spitting out
fumes of news and weather reports;
inducing people to blinker faces
with scarves and also glove
their hands like criminals.

A pair of exquisite thighs
make summer, he heard, whereas
cold had long been gnawing
at his marrow through tattered trousers.

As coins cease to hibernate in
his eroded palms, he rips out
pages of the universe and lights
fire for warming up to the latest.

The glowing tabloids neon headlines
about a president and then, in blackness,
soar into the sky like a kite....
That's all for now, goodbye....

Viva La Cats!

NU Wild Cats are so nice
they'd even toss a picnic with mice.

13Ft 3In Benson Ave.

Over here, a midnight snow-confetti juxtaposes
sun rays drizzling over bridal home soil.
A crystal half-moon entices my pining heart to crawl
over glistening rail tracks; save that raging wheels
sever it and, it tumbles into a gaping Shell pump,
over there....

Dangling Facts

(To argue) that women are but umbilical cords
void of matter between their ears
implies you are dangling snouts
masturbating at 90^0 between your legs.

Open As Petals

Do not be bewildered if I wipe
off your blood-red lipstick from
my lips after you have kissed me
hi & bye for I am going south,
without doubt, to meet my fiancé.

Pruning Of Roses

Clip, clip, clip...he deprives
roses of their milk from
the earth's swollen breasts

Clip, clip, clip...tears flow
from the umbilical cords
He stuffs petals into the rifle's nozzle
and thrusts a stone in the hand
of a perforated child.

Gatsha, Scavenger of History

Gatsha shall not be called Shaka
for the souls he shreds
to pieces like a sadistic shark
shall haunt him like spirits
devoid of stoppage, salute!

I shudder to think how your life;
a shallow, empty, eerie shell
smouldering on unknown shores, shall
be squeezed and swallowed
by the swirling seas of tears
and blood, in South Africa.

Shall you not be invested into a sack
full of rats, snakes, cats and dogs
where your sinister spirit
will be scavenged into shreds
of history. Amen!

Waiting At Johannesburg Station

When tear-ducts of heaven split,
sobs of rain fall on pining expectations.
Unsuspecting people are caught
by a heavy drizzle: newspapers become
umbrellas, and all too soon seem
to be covered from discomfort,
save the poet's rubble of flesh.
Howling wind hisses to the marrow
of scorned flesh. But this sprout
will gasp to its end, and birds
will sing to the rainbow —

Here comes a mouth full of golden kisses.

Children Of Zwepe

The clang of a spinning
coin is cupped by a hoping
hand. It screeches the coin
against the surface to solicit
a bet: head or tail?

The cooing of the night-bird
murmurs in the glare of light,
to silhouette the squatting hope.

The broken circle rises
to nag the fortunate one.
To stir rage swirling
inside their hearts.

The deserted plate alone,
with a patch of blood;
hopeful of yet another massage
when the children of zwepe wake up.

After a Hide

On a Sunday afternoon,
Twenty-two adults, myself included, chase
an inflated hide for a hundred rands.

Earth stampeded, roasts us as we chase
the ball. It is cheering and jeering outside
and panting and limping inside.

Us, trailing one nil, kick
as hard as ostriches to win
the game and hugs and kisses.

The following morning, I was
greeted by sore green toe-nails.

Wishes on Lines

My wishes flap over a washing line
like a parachute blown to skyline
by horns of stratification. Soaked
hands of a washer-woman also soar
far beyond billowing scrum shirts
like a rugby ball over poles
anchored onto genocidal lines.

Patrick Fitzgerald

Renegade Blues

For Karl Niehaus and Jansie Lourens

Returning Exile Psycho-Babble Blues

He returns to strange silence and the odour of death
He returns old, bald and forgotten
He returns with his briefcase bulging with blueprints
He returns with magazines loaded with ammunition
He never returns because he has dissolved or else is dead

His friends greet him in jubilant celebration
He is drunk with welcomes and the wine of his own earth
He is drunk and alone at an airport bar
He parades through the streets of his home town
He watches the parade from the back because
He has returned secretly

He is offered a professorship in political literature
He is offered a spare-room for the week
He is a troublesome returned exile needing a job
He is an annoying busybody telling people what to do
He is without a career or clear references
He is a veteran without a veto

A party is arranged and he is overwhelmed with emotion
A party was suggested but everybody is busy
He is interrogated as to what party he will be joining
For a while he is invited to dinner parties
But he cannot go because he is still in exile

He recognises the place, the waiter is still the same
He cannot find the old shebeen
Table mountain has been moved 50 kilometres west
Into the sea in an attempt to take it to America
He knows the streets but they no longer care about him
Still nothing matters as long as he is home

He returns to cheering but nobody offers a pension
He has no pop-up toaster, only a pistol
He arrives late on the property market
And applies to be allocated a typewriter
He has completely forgotten
The highveld lightening and thunder

He buys a C.V. cheap from someone leaving for Australia
At last he is elected to a committee
But lacking courage he is still in Europe

He drives in from Botswana through Transvaal mealiefields
He arrives from Namibia, wild as the coast
He takes a train from Mocambique through lush Natal
He comes in from Swaziland stopping at waterfalls
He takes a cruise and disembarks at Durban
Thinking *Luanda is beautiful, but this is our humidity now*
He stumbles into Cape Town, he arrives at P.E.,
East London welcomes him,
He leaves the ship at Richards Bay
He says, *Now at least we can change*
These damn colonial names
His ashes are scattered surreptitiously in Johannesburg
Since he never returns alive

He survives departure
He survives aids
He survives commando raids
He survives malaria
He survives parenthood
He survives new technologies
He survives promotion
He survives exile
But he doesn't return having lost his politics

Of course he returns he is incomplete elsewhere
Of course he returns for reconstruction
Of course he returns, so long prepared for it
As a disciplined cadre he returns when ordered
And he *must* return to be with the ghosts
Of those who died so that *he* might return

And knowing it will never be the same
That walking inside him will be
The years of walking elsewhere
The strange foods and the strange languages
Those other lands with their own beauty
Those other places with their own torment
Where he was although he was really always home

All that flesh insubstantial now
All that concrete and steel just tricks of light
All those hours that blew past him
When he was becalmed
All those years working the wheel
All that evidence against his return
Boiled down to nothing

And knowing then on his way through the airport
his small suitcase glued to his hand
containing all those years of absence
varied and intricate in themselves
at once wonderfully light and horribly heavy
knowing then that even if he's finally made it
there will be no individual coming back
there can be no personal return
the years have passed and the comrades have fallen
and return is unbitter only for the yet unborn

So what can he be doing now
awaking from a dream of returning
or dreaming of that time away from home

Oxford 1987

Fragment

I promised myself the right to write
about this time, one golden morning
still wanting to believe that I'll look back
upon these days with all that love
which once seemed expended

then there will be a whole full day
with no new exile
and we'll pick our way forward
through the bones, epitaphs and dreams

Johannesburg-Gaborone-Lusaka-Liverpool 1979-1990

Renegade Blues

(A Sectarian Talking Blues)

Seeing that most of us live day by day
and only a few impala-leapers
hurl themselves across weeks and months
across borders, fences, roads and seas
across drought and across hunger
from the one past to the multiple future....

what can we say, we pedestrians
stuck into the ground like thornbushes
eyed-out by these people and their cattle
too dumb to order ourselves a drink
too paralyzed to know fear

a gun in trained hands is knowledge
its hinges and oily places as intimate as a lover,
but now we must fight with bare-hands
against the monstrous spectacle of wasted time

Reading the newspapers we hardly even
look between the lines,
what happened to the times when our talking made sense
each newly lit conversation making ash out of the enemy,
and what happened to our leaders,
and what happened to our friends

hard men have taken over,
we are no longer consulted —
or hard women for all we know
for we know nothing anymore
except this purple night and beyond it
the rotting pumpkin of our spirit

that chair, plastic and empty,
these cigarettes, those glasses, that brooding waiter,
all these things make us suspect each other
we feel it like the damp sweat running down our backs
one of us will soon be turning traitor
leaving us here alone

and joining the movement

Gaborone 1983

Anticipation

I know
that each hour cannot wait for tomorrow
as each plan cannot wait to be perfect
as each comrade must grow older
keeping courage and keeping faith

for each exile is an exile of sorrow
and each exile an exile of lovers
and each memory a strange cloudburst
of water and light on a parched veld

I cannot know where I will be tomorrow,
eating unfamiliar fruit among new companions
or standing on guard or lying in ambush,
but a huge land is awaiting the return of her children
mountains beckoning, crops waving,
factories humming in anticipation
of that day of victory
of all our people free

Gaborone 1980

Those Who Got Lost

Gradually what actually happened
no longer belongs to those who happened to be there
the images are reproduced in photographs
on calendars, in a thousand well-intended publications
in a hundred not well-intended publications
its energies feeding that mournful monster
the western press
the media fattens and reproduces lies
until some of the people themselves
seeing themselves among the crowd, declare
'that's how it was'
and watch themselves being photographed,
their memory of the event fading
as their hopeful youth fades also
caught in a million media mirrors,
out of place, out of touch, out of time,

the struggle buried in unread (and unreadable) pamphlets
they become slaves to their own past
prisoners of time,
reactionaries.

Gaborone 1979

Those Who Did Not Get Lost

we remember those days as if they were yesterday
we know yesterday will never become tomorrow
we must never allow imperialism to ration us our own history
our knowledge is our revolution.

Gaborone 1983

Learning to Fight

Nowadays the anger is harder
those throwing stones no longer look behind them
those in prison gaze carefully at the sky
those without dreams systematically bolt windows
and even poets are learning how to fight

take heart brothers, a fierce wind is blowing south
take heart sisters, there are guns enough for all
our lizard rulers have basked enough in the sun
and we have filled up the cracks in the rocks with petrol.

Gaborone 1979

Militant

the militant wakes with iron filings on his hands
perhaps he has been making bullets in his sleep
he washes his hands and eats
perhaps today he must organise or fight
the militant enters the crowded streets
perhaps she works a full day in the factory

he is leaning on his rifle under a strange moon
he is reading by candlelight aloud
he is making love to someone he will never see again

after the tenth day without food
she fainted in the courtyard
the interrogation bruises showed underneath her smock
the hunger-strike still did not break

the militant tunes in the voice of his people
without breathing he follows codes beneath the static
today she will recruit her best friend
tomorrow he must leave the land he loves

Gaborone 1979

Urban Guerilla

casual in the bright day
careful in the wild night
he is there
not running
but resting on rock

he is there
new rumour among the shadows
simple justice against the power

Gaborone 1983

Exile

remember the friends gone
remember the days past
remember the moments that never worked themselves into poems

remember the necessary struggle

Gaborone 1979-1983

Bontleng Blues

For Hannchen

I am living without you now
a string of goats
having eaten my files

In the morning I see
an old cow
has been hit by a car
and milked dry

I do not think
the chickens in the yard
can tell us apart
when they're in a flap

Perhaps a dog should be heard
whining at my knee
or scratching restlessly
on the floor

but I see your cat
eats lizards and birds
and grows fat

walking through doors
I see it's because
I'm old hat

Gaborone 1979

Marina

No canals cross this Kgalagadi
without you my body is dry as desert
in a heat where only scorpions embrace

In the corners of my eyes, as the sun dances
I see you sparkling, through liquid diamond

Cattle wander across the Leidseplein
and cathedrals rear up among Jwaneng rock

my hands stretch out across koppies and cactuses
my tongue is swollen with words of longing
my mind is full of photographs of you

Gaborone 1983

If You've Gone
For Judy

find me on the corner
cigarette lit
I'll be alive
and I'll be alright

ash and smoke
define our path
I'll walk down it darling
iron in my heart

turn all the pages
of the book of lust
no definitions
will catch us up

Gaborone 1983

On Merseyside Missing Carolyn

impis of clouds defeat anaemic slivers of light
an exhausted season limps through this old port
remembering slaves ferried to a 'new' world
while deserted docks and cathedrals
parade their ravages in the interrupted sunset

above the satellites glide through
their complicated mathematical formulae
humming nonsense rhythms of nuclear holocaust
while melodious drunks stagger
from spaced-out railway carriages
but now I cannot master
the technologies of memory and distance

your absence is like a liquid I cannot pour away
opaquely revolving
crumbling endlessly
at the edges
like mirrors burning within mirrors

and what if a great thunder rolls somewhere
over the highveld
reeking of cordite and rain
and what if
the shift is changing on a Witwatersrand goldmine
with clangs of cages and gumboots' crunch
and what if the boats are returning
overflowing crayfish at Hout Bay
my history melts into geography
and still I'm missing you

for tenuous as sabotaged highways
my spirit tendrils reach for you
to cross the times between the times I'll
be with you
as pylons race across the windows of my
need for you

O love I need you with me,
palpable
to hold with every thought I'm capable
then as my only heart beats into you
you're all the people that I ever knew

Liverpool 1986

Ballad of the Green Coat
(or Confessions of an Albino Activist)

I met my comrade green coat in 1972
starting out short-haired
just finished call-up in Bloemfontein
and the whine of armoured cars still in my ears
which hadn't yet heard where the ANC was formed,
the green coat wasn't quite new either
demobilized from some other grisly army
probably the US retreating from Vietnam
a kind of marine greatcoat
with marks where the stripes had been fixed
four rand to your man in the shop
got a good greatcoat in Braamfontein
there it hangs behind the door
with two great big pockets
which held bottles of wine and still buttoned up
room enough for stolen books
poetry and philosophy in those scholar's times
shoplifting ourselves to an education
pockets of ideas to change the world
bohemian rhapsodies and wild scenes
first 'Free Mandela' (written on my first ballot form)
first lady and first love
all tumbled together
like the green coat on the backseat of a beat-up Ford,
that coat knew Hillbrow better than its own lining
whether Romano's or the German Beerhall
and the Chelsea Hotel (in Jo'burg, not the other one)
at the pavement cafes
old refugees from central Europe playing chess
reading Jaspers in German and Sartre in French

under the shadow of our own old Nazis

All night shopping at Fontana

nexus of a scrappy universe

where the bits and pieces of our society

jumbled together without self-consciousness or shame,

the blurred equality of the late night streets

the sudden non-racialism of the early hours of the morning

auguring another South Africa

so many things already on the make now

the metaphysical days nearly over

new times on the boil,

in the winter of 1976 with a green coat

marching mid-June over Queen Elizabeth Bridge

black-bereted in that children's revolution of hope

blood on the streets, blood in my mouth,

and first taste of jail

Highveld rain later at the lawcourts,

black beret charged, greencoat acquitted

lawyers requesting their fee

low assets, low equity,

belting up at the waist then

into a new time, a new tenure

on the move across the country

untested in a revolution

whose antiquity and grace

we didn't begin to comprehend

youth, courage and foolishness in a new mantra

Amandla for the new dawn

expected tomorrow at the latest

subversive cars carrying the green coat across the country

golden dawns over black asphalt

a hundred campaigns

a thousand badges on those broad lapels

not real badges like afterwards in exile
but the erotic cadences of our actions and emblems
three colours decorating our hearts
avante garde perhaps, but not yet trendy
storming into the towns and cities
with lives like pamphlets off a roneo machine
hammering into a big country
veld to veld, sea to sea
and greencoat came to know Cape Town
collar turned up against the drizzle
roving down Long Street or Lower Main Road
later Woodstock, Langa, Athlone, Guguletu
an old church left standing in the District
and *'you are hereby detained under section 22*
of the General Law Amendment Act'
such gobbledygook, *'Can I take my coat?'*

O well, too long a story,
just a few years
and a green coat crosses the border into Botswana
in an armoured car (one newspaper reported)
not true though good for a laugh
just one army greatcoat: green
into the indefinite plains of exile
into the ambiguous thighs of the future
into a new ball game, another contest
against the doubt in your own heart whether
your coat was really cut for these masks and tasks
no more wine in the pockets now
maybe a Makarov, beautiful in its own way, though who
can carry a gun and not sometimes think
of turning it on themselves

thank god it nestled so deep in those green cavernous pockets
along with all the codes and the secret messages necessary
to bury your heart in Gaborone rhythms,
five years with a coat on the edge of a huge desert
knowing enemy weapons would come one day or night
so many times waking in naked terror (for nothing)
until inevitably,
as the dam above the village bursts, or the bile
in a rotten appendix
the commandos finally come
and into the earth go the comrades
shall we name some streets after them
in the new South Africa then?
along with those shot down namelessly in the townships
those who slipped away anonymously
in the resettlement areas
or those dealt with by the death squads
so long as sorrow can be allowed to burst its own seams
(now Mandela says it's reconciliation road)

well the green coat wasn't collared
safe in Lusaka
bullet holes avoided
standing guard with magazines in the pockets
or out and about, fulfilling its multifarious purposes
as the icy wind whips off Amsterdam canals
driving it to hang about in a warm cafe
coffee and alcohol, rich tobacco
or wending the London streets
searching again for bookshops
after all this time
even seeking out Mayakovsky's residence

the wonder of a brass plaque on a house in Moscow,
joining words to places
or crunching on the Norwegian snow
toward an old historic church
up a hill where the Swedish invader was defeated
hundreds of years ago, forming a nation
other people's history, who now support our struggle
a green coat discarded in sultry Rio
Brazil a parallel-universe South Africa
home and not home
a sensuous whiff of what didn't come to be,
or left lying on the bed
through a long drinking night in Luanda
Angolan beer and Cuban rum
dodging home after the curfew
quite certain our bodies are magic
against those friendly bullets of our MPLA allies
the moist thick air like Durban's
when you sweat after a good curry,
but green coat was somehow always ahead
that little bit extra up its sleeve
trimmed better to the road back to the future
winding itself around me, saving me
from that bleak enchantment of the ill-loved
sirens of cold grandmother Europe
one cold night on the Pont Mirabeau
over the Seine
those deep pockets reminding once again
how love always did follow after pain

well there's no point in naming all the places
green coat wasn't really a tourist
more of a part-time combatant and pavement connoisseur
right through all these other worlds
some full of the most expensive coats and hats
like Geneva, one great big department store
others full of people needing coats and
other things much more than coats and Swiss watches
like houses, education, peace
and soldiering on, comrade green coat,
from Maputo and Dar es Salaam
landing up at last in another port city
this time a cold one of past glory
once spewed out piss poor immigrants to the new world
whose great-great-grandchildren now run the show in
Washington, New York, Auckland, Sydney, Jo'burg
once working class and starving farmers
transfigured by some stock exchange hidden hand,
bygone wealth at the tip of the slave triangle
great buildings of stone built on the proceeds
of humans subjugated on plantations
old fashioned ships setting out over grey waters
for Africa, still exploited in 1990
while a Beatles tune is humming inside the coat
and a chilly wind whipping up off the Mersey,
guaranteeing the hard days night
with pockets full of magazines again
(the kind with articles, not the kind with bullets)
and a box of floppy disks fitting in easily
such a glut of data in such a small place
where will it all end
this headlong progress

from ignorance to stupidity,
old green coat sceptical of scholarly pursuits
leers from a coat-stand in a seminar room
grimaces in the sleet on the way to the library
drips shabbily over the warm heater
laughs slyly into its buttons
snuggles up next to a warm television, which coughs
then suddenly announces
'Mandela is free, what the hell are you doing here?'

I take a good look at my companion coat,
all the stitches and stains,
what will they think at Jan Smuts Airport
you know, the customs and immigration officials
sniffing at some bright,
newly issued green mamba of a passport
noticing the wearer, so lacking a suntan
wan, nothing to show for all those years
except a loaded lap-top computer
booted-up, laced up for this sudden new future
bulging with useless post-Fordist data
and a green army coat, terribly out of fashion,
and 'can you explain....,' your man is asking
'well this coat never was in fashion sir'
I hope I'll answer wittily, through my tears.

Liverpool 1990

Phedi Tlhobolo

Ten Pretoria Dub Poems
and a Lament

Teardrop Dub

How many times
the voice of a peasant boy?
How many times
the cry of a slave mother?
How many times
our pain from your doings?

Imagine
where you would be
if the earth was small
and you living alone
we gone

My life is but a polluted sea
a river preserved for its smelling fish
you suffocated my future
with injustice and a colourbar
hence my loneliness in your visions

How many times
must I shed a tear
in my own land?
Night vigils and bullet wounds:
How many times?

Imagine
what life would have been
without my music and culture
that you stole
to give birth to your culture

My life is but a broken hill
that stands between the breath of nature
conquered and disused
like a diamond field in Kimberley
forgotten and outcast
as if it had never been there before

How many times
must I go silent like the night
my voice in shame
enduring strife and tribulations?
How many times as you grow rich and fat
must I wait
in this stinking ghetto?
How many times
in my dreams
the revolution and the police?
How many times
a teardrop on my face?

How many times the stealing of life
and the outlaw of the truth?
I can't take this any more
Soweto can't any more
Pretoria can't any more
none of us can any more
How many times do we have to fall
senseless as fighting bulls?

How many times
South Africa?
Your ignorance is killing me
kicking me to death
Oh Pretoria
how many times
do I have to write sad poems
while other poets write love songs?

Dub for Time

Too much
working
in the city
for a quantity
coin
no food
no life
but sweating
in this
fellah country

Time passing by
like the sun
from the east
the rain from above
months passing
years going
no child
no life
no freedom
in this fellah city

Time
bastard time
bloody time
son of creation
I wonder why
my head goes bald
meanwhile time
goes young
there must be an
abnormality somewhere
between the bourgeoisie
the workers and
the peasants

Dub Message Rubbing

Call for your unity
as the stones did
roots above the leaves below
rivers dry but eyes flooded
communication rare
complications keep cropping up
call for your growth
and go green as the golf course

I Dub for You

In the language of the birds
I prefer the singing trees
whispering the lyrical lines of a poet
to the silent ants and voiceless pythons
a sweat drop quenches the thirst
raindrops molest our corn
listen to the clarion call
of never ending values
dub messages rubbing the tail of a lion

Dub dub
as you dip your nose in dope
Dub dub
as you double your doom with dope
Dub dub
as you slip into a dubious dubbin
away with a demented mind
dread fools sing as you go bald
for you no longer belong to a soul

It's Friday night
pass me I pass you
the annoyed ears of heaven
waits for first-aid
Aids aids population control
emergency death
no man must weep for such spiritual departure
Dub as they dub on you

Explore the reason
of facts finding
exploding the fear shell
if you do the dubbin debate
prey on your dubious problems
such days do come
when the poet's voice goes drowsy
but the dub message explodes even
in our dreams

Dub dub
as you win by God's will
Dub dub
as death tramples on you
Dub dub
as we go for purity and spiritual
quality
dub as I move your feet
with the rubbin dub message

Beast Dub

There goes a man
hairy as a lion
brandishing a weapon of war
coming to my home

he is a beast of steel
employed to maim and mutilate
he is an animal

There he is
caged in a police force
annoyed by peaceful silence
entertained by the cry of anguish

he is a beast of steel
employed to maim and mutilate
he is an animal

There he goes
hopeless and unsure
sheltered in a lone stupor
isolated from humanity

He is a beast of steel
employed to maim and mutilate
he is an animal

There he goes
biting the hand that feeds him
programmed to kill and steal
going to Palestine to plunder
to Lusaka against the people
to South Africa against himself

there he is
confused and dreamless
that man is a beast of steel
in the image of a human being
employed by satanic states
he is an animal
ready to kill and steal

He is a beast of steel
coming to kill and steal
he is the beast
the traitor
the rapist
the betrayer
he is the animal

Stop the war....
Stop the bloody killing

Why do you fight
when you have voices   X2

Those bombs you design
against the people on earth
are not necessary
people need food not doom

Why do you fight
when you have voices   X2

Destroy this gifted world
tomorrow you will float
in the sea of shame
like a snake you will be homeless

Why do you fight
when you have voices   X2

Why when you have voices
why stage a destruction
campaign

Those technologies of doom
polluting the air we breathe
leads us nowhere
atomic bombs have no proteins
only radiation

Why do you fight
when you have voices   X2

Politicians, teachers
teach the children the truth
abandon fictions
better talk of solutions

(repeat chorus and fade)

Hard Lines Dub

Still the fruits are raw
me and you crossed
birds mate
man maim
across the bridge
down the horizons
as I weep
the earth awaits me

I work the gardens
my master runs a brothel
he is a high class creature
I eat the left-overs
I can't buy a hot-dog

The SATV yesterday
announced a new period
war is over
all guns are down
Reaching out to clean my hair
I discover that
this freedom is not for me

The fruit is still not ripe
and the prisons are not empty yet
All I know is that
the birds are mating
the earth is waiting.

I am Yesterday Dub

I am yesterday
when bullets
fell on the ground
like monsoon rains.
I am yesterday

I am yesterday
when the bowels of the earth
greedily consumed man
I am yesterday

I am yesterday
when running for her life
a mother's leg broke
I am yesterday

I am yesterday
when Namibia like a tortoise
was skinned alive
I am yesterday

I am yesterday
when at home they sang,
'mayibuye iAfrica-Pambili ngomzabalazo'
I am yesterday

I am yesterday
when the comrades toyi-toyied at Nasrec House
defying the regimes of a dying era
I am yesterday

I am yesterday
go tell it on the mountains
the son of the bitch is alive
I am yesterday

I am yesterday
a day in the life of man
the more I run the more I fall
I am yesterday

I am yesterday
when fools died
for want of wisdom
I am yesterday

I am yesterday
when purple rain
fell on us in the ghetto
I am yesterday

I am yesterday
when our dreams dimmed
and our days were dull
I am yesterday

I am yesterday
when Dr. Verwoerd
named Africans, Kaffir baboons
I am yesterday

I am yesterday
when the rent boycott
resulted in a bloody war
I am yesterday

I am yesterday
when a school boy prisoner
died in the veld
I am yesterday

I am yesterday
the day I will never forgot
it burnt into my body
I am yesterday

I am yesterday
the life I lived
is the life a people lived
I am yesterday

I am yesterday
I belong to the trampled
souls of the many
I am yesterday

I am yesterday
when the toilets of Africa were painted
'Europeans only'
I am yesterday

I am yesterday
when my colour
was high treason
I am yesterday

The Sound Keeps Sounding Dub

From time immemorial there was a sound
and the sound goes on

at home
I meditate
to nourish my soul

and the sound goes on

in your sleep
you travel in a dream
to the far horizons of your destiny

and the sound goes on

we march in defiance
with visions of redemption
our feet dancing
to the rhythm of a kwela song

and the sound goes on

I never learned
not to be vindictive
even when time is against me
in victory my spirit lingers
like the echo of marabi blues

and the sound goes on

I have a dream
to walk on the carpet of liberty
in defiance against inhumanity
my struggle goes on
and the sound keeps sounding.

Down the Road Dub

I no longer sing harmonies
of my generation
with that voice admired
by babies in their sleep

Half of that I used to do
no longer exists
in me only anthems of solitude
amuse the veins

I am not of the Kwela times
but of nuclear decades
I go in the yawning air
for meditation
between me and creation
there is a road of polished electric tears

Down the road
as I drift along
a gunshot echoes
for your briefing
calamity is no more
but, its gravel voice still reverberates

Damn the Law Dub

Hear dem talking on the lines
plotting espionage with imperial swines
CIA bullets inna USA.
the whisper of the Koevoet
down inna SA
community inna de blood

The world inna blood
community dying
the people inna flood
the nation crying

Hear through the call
the Klan is running to the fall
the collapse of a kingdom
FBI bullets inna Africa
the revolution rumour inna Pretoria
the world inna de blood

Nasty Change Dub

Wasted efforts
the land narrowed by graves
and the living drowned in blood
no forward going
it's backwards every time

guns of steel
embrace death like a friend
steel could build islands of leisure
not threaten peace and kill

We Dread the Burning Sun Dub

I cannot surrender
nor leap from my soul
in honour of disguised change
to wholesale peace
at the market of dispossession

Days Numbered Lament

In this time of transition
a new spiritual world is singing
unto the young
the old
and the late
for now bliss becomes our day
while behind the hills
a depraved luxury fades
the days of our suffering
are numbered

I stand unshaken
the rays of hope spreading over me
but, like one bereaved
I still wail for my history

Who knows
the fate of man
like the earth knows the moon?

In this land
of bleeding hands
freedom,
like a baby
is being born!

Rustum Kozain

Desire for the Sun

Love Song

I have sung my Arcadian odes
and my lyrics of love,
and I have moaned my ballads of resentment,
but I have not wept your elegy,
for in me lies the seed straining at re-entry,
the latent beauty of agonised dreams,
waiting to burst upon the soil and spill
the seeds of rebirth.
Now I must sing the ultimate love song.

I

    The day is done.
The mountain shadow reaches across the sprawling richness,
brisky cool in the autumn late afternoon lassitude,
and a shiver runs down my spine:
on a clear day you see the shadows
touch-touching the Cape flats,
then the sudden all-engulfing
with the cool coldness of dusk
bringing fire to the sky.

    In the ivory tower
the goose pimples come quicker, larger,
and the pit-pat of foreground tennis,
fails to reflect my contentment
like water falling into a fulfilled bowl.
Instead, I shiver,
while the tennis players defy the chill
with aggressive arrogance,
and walkers walk their dogs —
genuine leather leash and all —
over smoothly cut, well-looked-after lawns.

I shiver, because,
on a clear day you can see the Cape flats
and imagine it where it sprawls over sand,
under wind;
where dust grinds your smiles
into grimaces that overshadow the joy of labour.
On a clear day you can see the haze over the townships,
pressing heavily down, choking,
whirling and mixing oppressively with the dust,
and the distinctive sound of sand grains
blown against tin, cardboard and plastic.
I shiver, in the late afternoon:
the joy of labour exists not there....

II

Even I cannot, in my shaky song,
recreate your rhythmic hammering,
nor can I paint your corrugated palms,
but I can smell your sweat,
your cheap-wine-stained breath:
in it I find no apple blossoms,
nor freshly hewn hay
no sweet smell of work.
And I must break from lyrical yearning
where workers move as if in a dream,
sowing peaceful seeds,
children gaily dancing in crisp white clothes.
I must break from this
and paint the blood that drains the sky of possibilities,
drained in painful labour that groans and grinds

and gives birth to helpless fists,
flailing, trailing ancestral entrails
over the harrow of defeat.

    Bear me away, then,
before I drown in this quagmire of history.
Let the night be witness
and take me where the new dawn shivers
with embryonic eagerness,
where the pain of labour,
the sweat from angry brows,
the blood from cracked palms,
fuse into a mass of movement,
a shout: No more!
Let me sing, in stark metaphors,
of workers not at peace,
no idyllic Arcadias,
but the gravel playgrounds growing glass-shards,
and the questioning child before the onslaught
of the yellow monsters.
Let these be my metaphors:
bottle, stone
clearcut and violent
like a nightmare riddling the contented evening.
Let these be mine.
I cannot write of the night that's evil,
for I have evoked its blackness
to bear witness
to my birth.

III

    The morning clarity escapes the Cape Flats,
the smoky haze caught under the cold,
the burnt out residue of night.
From here I cannot fathom the ache.

IV

    Somewhere, beyond this tower,
a jumble of shacks,
hidden from the national (embarrassment) road,
have long since creaked goodbye
to their occupants well on their way
to a heartless parent city — the joy of labour.

    In sour rain-soaked clothes,
with faces dour and rippled — canyons of pain —
limbs aching a quiet tiredness — the joy of labour.
And your eyes flicker resentment at this joy.
The virtue of labour dangles like a rotten carrot,
where the strain of muscles,
the ache of bones,
and sweat that sears the eyes,
bring knowledge of pain,
where beady eyes question
the high-voltage buzz speeding overhead,
while weary feet crack beneath the sharp pang of firewood,
piercing into the shoulders,
bringing a forceful knowledge
that lies bubbling before dawn.

The train rattles past undulating golf courses,
well kept lawns that lie and rot all week.
And houses voice their opinions
towards the third-class life
that stares in longing at each house,
different as their owners want.
You shuffle your thoughts to re-address the issue,
to address it in such a way
that you know the meaning of revolution:
we don't want to play golf here.
We want to rip up the fields and build houses.
Rip up the fields with wanton,
destroy, destroy
the smooth richness and turn over the sods
to show up dark brown in its richness,
to sow seeds in these weals and sprout dissent.
The golf courses must go.

Flashback memories feed the anger
until destruction beckons seductively,
with whispers of untold possibilities.

Imagine, Jameson Hall in flames,
purifying flames that lick the sky.
that sear the sensitivities
which are pampered by succulent exercises of intellect.

The afternoon colours the sky
in opium-flavoured encouragements,
whispering twilight pleasures
to hate-blind eyes and calloused hands,
and cigarettes raped, onto the filter,
as the train halts and movements change
to crass colours billowed on the smell
of neatly wrapped fish-and-chips
that'll grease the slogan channels....
third-class smells carry the world
in a maddening twirl of anger.

The radicals are exploring
all decolonised avenues of subversion.
And the liberals,
they grimace at the prospect,
silently contemplating the ethics of it all.
After the battle they return
to their rich-African-decor houses,
sighing content
as they peacefully settle down in big warm beds,
smiling at their victory in the recent debate:
rational, humanist and ethical.

The rain drums soothingly on the tile roofs.
Outside the cold lurks.

V

Tonight the cold rushes through,
unseen.

The evening paints you blue-black
in moonful gulps of fear,
whispering the secret pleasure of hardened hearts,
dripping crimson concrete to build a fragile night,
as you stalk the muddy webs
to where the cauldron simmers,
gathering all the anger into bottles of liquid danger.

Imagine, Jameson Hall in flames.

Tonight you must imagine the cold earth,
the cold rain.
Imagine, out there,
beyond,
where you can see nothing,
out there is a seething mass of mud and death.

The slogans slide securely into the potted despair,
the hammers sweep sickly,
like fists beating the frightful air,
and you cast your hand
in scary, unsure slight,
to feed the fire from afar.

1989

Revolutionary II

How could we explain this,
this feeling that blows through,
through the cold saxophone furrows of our souls?
This feeling that coils around the blisters,
the blisters we thought had healed?

Feel how they burn here,
here in the dampened amber-glow
the glow that the candles paint,
etching deeper into the furrows,
the weals of discomfort
that fret,
slow,
quick quick,
fretting incessantly:

Your fingers know their pain
and the guitar whines through the glow,
moans and whines,
then frets and picks,
razor sharp,
resenting this feeling.

We Were Moving Northwards

We were moving northwards, out into a sprawl
             of black rock,
while other epics lay crumbled like wet serviettes;
things down south were bad, all talking, belching,
                     gasoline refugees,
and songs of prowess drawn from wells dug from rocks.
We lost our grip time and again,
saw our pleasures whisper away into a cold northern dawn;
our worlds crumpled:
frosted flowers shivered in the gaze of ancient reptiles,
but we pushed on.
Our clothes clung,
our skins taught,
and the further north we moved, the lighter we became;
the smell of angels and rock, dust and aloe, moonlight:
these were the smells of our love.

We were free from the questions of our past,
so we could move faster,
shaking dust into another dawn,
brushing hats and coats;
free from dust, we moved again, always northwards, always;
our hands down, swinging to a new rhythm,
our hair flames to gods:
those who would stay with us
in a murder, ruthlessly, of innocents.

In a gully we came upon a scene,
a scene borne through the ages and which we thought
we had left behind;
we closed our eyes and prayed, our knees sunk into the
soft sand,
our ears trembling like bats,
our lives translucent geckoes with irregular pulse;
but after the ceremony, after the rituals were done,
we could do nothing but push on, northwards.

At dusk of another day our heads were heavy:
overripe fruit with chapped lips,
hungry hearts and thirsty hands,
and we fell to treachery:
clasping unknown knives in unknown ways,
our hands flashed an uncertain pattern
except that death was sure.

Returnings

I
Always returning,
we will wander through our mosque souls,
the cool cool tombs of secret longing.

The mountains tumble deep
inside the borders of my stream.

In the beginning we could laugh,
muddy feet,
me and you and us,
sleepily on the return

to tall cool grass
which grimaces through our fingers,
which hooks through our hair,
behind cooler corners of the houses;
we could,
with the meant grimaces of mad worms,
stroke our fingers over broken glass,
the cold gooseflesh a proof of love.

On abrasive concrete walls,
in the beginning,
we could feel the plunge of stolen fruit
deep within our throats,
and wipe the blood from our knees,
here in the shadows of lost parents.

In the beginning all the memories were
ghost-tracks and seeds;
all the memories were rugby-field dreams,
at lunch-break,
with sandwiches on barbed wire,
me and you and us;
the heroes of tomorrow's memories.

II
   Come come,
the road is long and hot,
I pray for rain
and you sleep your poet's dream.

Can we meet, against the slopes of a new mountain,
with the rush of (once again) granite
which leaves us helpless?

Come come,
the road is rocky and bloody
warm,
I pray for rain
and your words cut accurately.

III
In the beginning.

The absence was a dark pool,
deep underneath rock and fern,
the water yesterday in your eyes.

In the beginning the heartbeat was fast,
high up in the Boland mountains.
We were children watching snowflakes,
watching from inside old cars.

IV
Now that the metaphors are depleted....

V
Sweet, strong coffee
and the steam from our palms
outlined the ghosts of today,
stretched against the winter clouds
with the bass patterns of a father's voice.

In old cars,
in the beginning,
dad,
my dream began.

VI
    And it continues....

VII
    Come come,
it's late
and the road is high and cold,
come angel from words
and stroke me to rest
with your deeply buried, magic words.

Love Song II

My love burns through my gaze
that flutters over this dark soil;
my love burns for those mountains
and in those mountains
(hear the granite melt!)

Lead me to you;

My body is small and sacred,
but holds promises of redemption
as i enclose you,

mountain,
tree,
ants;
as I feel you scrape
a pine-needle song into my eyes.

The tears will not quench
the crackles of my cries,
nor the thirst of startled dassies,
but there'll be freedom in pyres
as I stretch across granite
to burn with this land.

In flames and smoke
we'll trace slogans on water,
across clouds,
and our bleary eyes will obscure
the blisters in our hearts.

Burn long and hard
(my life is black already),
through the hole in my gaze,
which no monolith can fill
but the sound of melting granite.

Burn, my land,
I lie on you,
dead and waiting for flames.

Suicide Note

When autumn comes
catch for me leaves,
crumple them
A fistful to your nose
and I will wipe a tear
from your eye.

Catch leaves for me
and twirl through your fingers
some spirits,
dance to rhymes
and breathe
while memory fades my death:
I'm gone from here
to paint the sky into its vision.

Catch for me leaves
and whisper words to my soul,
dance to rhymes
and remember my gaze brittle,
my palms soft
and my desire for the sun.

For Alicia

What can be said at all can be said clearly;
and whereof one cannot speak, thereof one must
be silent.

— Wittgenstein

How can I say that
you have angels on your tongue;
how can I say that
you hold granite in your fingers,
that you smear it across pages
and the pages curl into flames
scraping into my eyes;
that you know potholes of muddy water:
powder-blue sky,
clouds and rainbows and poverty
caught in these brown mirrors;
that you hold your fingers to ice
and the ice melts
under the weight of your words;
that your words are spider arcs,
cobwebs and dew,
icicles of absences
that call me to blue mountains?

Storm

Let this storm blow its darkness,
and howl;
Let it rip at my sinews,
tatter them into its own wind;
Let it enfold me,

totally in black
until I can feel it,
until I stumble wide-eyed into its grip,
its fingers clasping my arms;
Let it blow and tear at the fragility of my night:

I will return to your silent armpits,
to your pages arcing over me;
I will resort to that crinkling in my eyes,
I will return to your flecks upon my skin,
and the mad rush of blood to my finger tips
as I cajole you to answer me
with the leafy words conjured from a stormy night:

Memories are smoke, unstable in the storm,
momentary death every time your touch locks over me
and my words are trolleyed all the way down,
down,
down,
into your silent asylums.

Night, burn in me,
ragged laugh and whisper whisper
burn in me.

Things are not what we think,
this shadow not my own,
but my attendant,
faithful to the end,
pushing my trolley
and laughing with me
as we enter the bend.

I Taste You in the Shadowy Afternoon....

I taste you in the shadowy afternoon,
in the ruins of a hot day
as the colours of me raise their stringent laughter;
grey-blue and fragrant
like your sweat.
I run my charcoal gaze over your ridges,
over the curves that glide
taut to my anxiety.

This is then also where death finds me;
in the shadow of your armpit,
against the flow of your dress —
small deaths over and over
streaking the day.

In your silences
I come apart
limb by trembling limb,
breath by breath
and I strain against,
the marble of the sky,
bursting into an unsure flight.

Barbara Schreiner

Against the Skin-Grey Bark

Three Poems For A Sister In Jail

I. Song For Jenny

There's another bomb gone off
But no one flinches any more,
Our brothers are on the border
Fighting someone else's war,
But I've sniffed some kind of mythical glue —
Limitations blew apart:

I'm tunnelling under prison floors
With scuttling cockroaches the only wards
Of secrets whispered in detention night.
I slip between the cracks.

I hear the pages of her bible turn —
Mary still a virgin, Jesus dead.
Tomorrow MC squared will still be E
And us inside our jails.

But I've come to the war with plans in my head
For the spirit of the people here has led
The workers and the animals and me —
To come and get you out!

Come through with us into the moon's blue land,
Spread silver on your face and on your hands,
And leave your feet behind, we'll lend you wings
And the voice of an owl to prophecy your call.

II. For Sisters in Jail

Sister —
Let there be no regrets.
If tears must fall in lonely prison nights
Let them be vitriol
That scalds through years
Of convict-polished floors
To open up the pathways of resistance.

Sister-hero —
Do not doubt
That thousands know
That we must fight
To end this fighting.

Sister-woman —
Do not mourn.
Your sacrifice of unborn children
Will not be in vain.

Should walls turn into gelatine
And melt away,
And bars turn into sugar-sticks
In bored jailers' mouths,

Looking out from that small cell
They deem your world
You will see
Our children play
As yours,
Our mothers fight
As you,
Our sisters love
As us.

Sister —
Do not doubt that millions say
That we will fight
To end this fighting.

III. Between Two Loves

Like a kiewiet's wing
his fingers brush my throat
his eyes warm with vintage Meerlust
stroke my lips.

(Behind their jangled key-closed doors
I may not touch her,
fingers meeting soft as wild kapok
against the glass,
breath murdered by the strangling static
of an intercom.
Unsentenced yet
but sentenced not to touch.)

Breast touching chest
we pause —
in the hiatus between our passion
and the future.
I hold my fingers to your smiling warmth
until the graveyard touch of glass is gone
and fiery flamboyants begin to flower.

(Then, when the blazing risen sun
melds all our futures into one,
I will hold her bone-thin body
and warm it with the scent of wild olives
from him
        to me
          to her
through touch of skin on skin.)

I Must Not Call Your Name
For J.S.

I do not know you, (comrade) in their cage,
thinking of steel jaws closing and how long
can you stand barefoot on two bricks
naked, (your midnight body between my thighs)
in the heat, (we moved in love
while rain fell from the flame tree)
I do not recognise your face, turn aside
from prowling ears that stalk
my tongue (tasting our sensous flesh
we measured our brief time between the sheets
of revolutionary pamphlets to be written
and read) Blood stains the disembowelled house
where sirens bayed (in the disguising night
I came to you to kindle a future)
past the enfolding dark to open doors
(that ripens now inside my body)
I must not call your name
(but the drops fall) silent
as the shadows that cross my door
(and the spears of corn stand thick in the fields)

Cave

In the moist shade of ferns, the cleft widens,
seducing you with the silence of falling water
that breaks in steam on carved rock.
You tunnel between stone, your narrow beam
probing the dark water.

'Sheila 4 Harry' he scratched inside a heart
at the bottom of the biggest stalagmite.
Shifting now on the damp sheet he feels
her pulse pinned under his flaccid penis, sees
the red bruise starting at the base of her neck.

To Evelyn, On My Brother's Death

The bricks of the kitchen floor are smooth
like licked chocolate, under your feet.
Your starched apron holds in your grief
like ribbons hold together the flowers
that people send
and send
and envelopes hold the cards
'it was god's will'
that must be replied to
but how, when there are no words
to bind our broken scraps.
The bricks of the kitchen floor are warm
like melted chocolate
from the years you polished them
like you polished his glasses on your apron

then, when he dropped the chutney jar
which fractured like life breaks on tarmac,
and he cried in the pain of childish clumsiness.
No words now.
Only your starched apron pasting over the cracks
until I reach your grief into my arms
like you used to hold me in the evenings
when mum and dad were out —
the theatre? a meeting? dinner?
and the Indian mahogony creaked
with the presence of tokoloshes.
For all those years of 'tula mtanam'
I can bring no comfort now
for the son that wasn't yours
whose tackies no longer dirty your polished bricks,
whose hands no longer tug your apron edges,
whose search for knowledge took him far away
until the callous passing of a hit-and-run
left him in foreign soil, for ever.
And so, I hold you,
holding me,
and in the world there is only this moment
and us,
two women.
Underneath our feet the kitchen bricks are worn smooth
by the passing years.

Who Is He Whom We Applaud?

Six months alone
    beyond letters
      no mirror
     only their words
that they have stolen from us
to fill their mouths —
then one day
    he walked tall
from the beast's belly
and we sang for victory
    and the lion roared again
louder than before

     [but now at night
      he turns the mirror to the wall
       to hide the reflection
     of his Janus face]

We gave him the spear
picked from where it fell
that mislead night,
carved his name
upon the stages of our history,
    burned his words
     like graffiti onto our membranes.

    [but between the troubled eyes
    the mirror's cracked —
    he blocks the split
     with words, packed in with newspaper

before the truth leaks through
into his daytime face]

Now watching from the balcony
    I ask myself
       is it the Vivas and Amandlas
the roar of many breaths
      that shake the paper
in his hand?
I have felt his body tremble
leaf-like in the night.
    I have tasted his fears
      like sea-spray on my chest.
Do I imagine the quivering mirage
that swirls around the lion's roar
'They did not break me!
I am strong,
    stronger than ever before.'

    [but at night he cannot sleep
    feels the mirror warp and tear,
    the silver lining peeling
      like skin from a burned memory —
    what did he tell them?
    did they see him weep
    alone in his cell
    like a thief on his cross?
    — in the morning he will glue it back
    with words chewed up and spat out
      like he pastes the smile across his eyes
      before the sun is up]

Now,
an actor on a stage
trapped in the glare of lights,
in the roar of many voices,

> he sings of victory
> alone with his fears
> and his words stolen from the brave
> and his people.

Safe Circle

Three wild pear trees protect me
from your 'Baby,
come suck my balls!' and
obscene laughter in the street.
One bends in the breeze
behind my head,
one stands on either side,
tinkling frost-silver, spring-silver
umbikanyana, herald of the new season.
Simple leaves in the breeze
like chimes
until I cannot hear your voice
see only your extended mouth
in brutish violence.
But still the breeze is blowing
Blowing your words and lips away
Blowing your swollen penis from your cupped hand.

Umbikanyana,
three trees protect me
Frost-silver, spring-silver
Three wild pears protect my soul
Safe-soul in silver-sound
Three wild pear trees surround me.

For Tshidiso — Baby Girl

I
'She danced inside me, then got stuck
That's why her hand is bent like that.
Like that.
It may have been a disprin that I drank
to cure a tension headache
from my first-born daughter's death,
that's why her hand is bent like that.
Like that.
It's very rare   doesn't happen often
They'll operate   she'll learn to write
without a thumb.
She has some other blessing that we'll learn about
when she's a little older.
She's marked for something,
brings some special message to this world
that's why her hand is bent like that.
Like that.'

II

'What did I do
What did I not do
that brings this anger on me
In my child's hand?
What gift did I neglect
In what duty sin
To bring this pain on me
One daughter passed away
One daughter's hands both
Cripple?
Am I so much the child of Eve
That I must pay, and pay, and pay?
Am I bound with Nongqawuse's sex
To suffer?
And my daughters?
What did I do
What did I not do
That brings this anger on me
In my child's hand?'

III

'Little one, so prematurely small
your fragile fingers clasp without a thumb
around my finger.
I will be your thumbs,
your agile hands
until the orange tree has grown to fruit
and you have drunk its drops of gold
Then you will be your own hands
and I will be your friend.'

Umbokhoto

Listen to me,
you out there somewhere,
being men.
Bend your head towards the shape of my mouth.
I am woman.
Listen to these words
written in red
like the stained sheet
when first love comes together
like the once white shirt
of a sister raped and stabbed
behind the school
inside the car
beside her child.

Listen while I shout my words like thunderclouds
that swell like bruises across a sister's cheek
and block the light.
Ask yourselves
out there somewhere, being brothers,
how will the sun rise
the day dawn
when you have closed woman's eyes
with fists of anger
drunken boots.

I am woman.

Don't bring your anger home
to tear my skin
Don't let the daily hate
seep through your bones
to pound against my flesh.

Listen to me
out there, somewhere, being men,
I feel pain.
I am umbokotho.
I am woman.

Can Mantisses Pray?

Today I moved a pot plant
Interrupted
as I thought
two mantisses, mating.

Like some steroided weightlifter
she clasped his body
in one serated leg
folded double like monstrous pliers
his back legs waving feebly
in and out in helpless mode
Then I saw
the pleasure of their intercourse
had been over
some time before I interrupted
— the first course, fresh mantis leg
had been eaten.

As I watched she leaned
triangular head
towards
triangular head
pale sea-green   towards its match
and nibbled
no, ground her relentless mandibles
into his eye

Some years ago I learned —
in some post coital hunger
the mantis eats her mate
crunching his crusty shell
like one might savour
cream-filled vol-au-vent
in the best of restaurants

But today I saw it.

Today   I shuddered at the sight
of like consuming like
of a lover   not yet dead
devoured from the extremities
inwards

The female mantis   lacking consciousness
does what her instinct orders
The male   lacking speech
submits without complaint.
And the human observer
anthropomorphising
philosophising
analysing
is shocked.

To An Ex-Lover

I
That thing you've dismembered
put away in your internal cupboard
like stacks of tinned cat-food
or bags of rice pocked with weavil holes
is me

that loose end you've tied up
into a Gordian knot
and bundled into the dark
where not even I can see myself
is me

not just two eyes   full of hurt
heavy thighs   a moist cunt
laughter   a tendency to quick anger
mountain walker   poet
a memory
but me   whole
alive and in pain
playing the guitar strings of normalcy
smiling   cooking for friends
working   writing
weeding   watering
being woman
weeping
healing myself with what powers I know

and you?
you churn in the pit of my stomach
like mephistopheles
till I throw up
avocado and brown rice
burning my throat like brimstone

I will not eat   until you die
a starved rat in a forgotten laboratory
where science is no more
nor art
nor heart
nor life

And I will play the guitar strings of normalcy
smile   cook for friends
work   write
weed   water
heal myself with what powers I know
and be wholly woman.

II
Open the door
not the front door   that's too easy
the little silver one
the one with the handle so small
it makes your fingers clumsy
Peer inside
there   the middle drawer
open it   see
the bruised stain on the bottom
purplish   like old blood?

that's my soul
remember?
the one you bought assiduously
night   after sultry night
smiling

close it now
put it away

the top drawer seems a little open
pull it wider
there   that pile of feathers
that's my trust
remember?
you asked for it
like down from the breast of a swan
and I gave it
but the swan   bare-breasted
died
without a song

close it now
put it away
hide the stains some dripping water made

the bottom drawer?
need you open it?
can you recognise that shredded mound
like cotton waste
so changed now from when you begged me
'just let me love you'

close the drawer
carefully now
as one walks in the presence of death
tiptoe

III
I have a cupboard of fun
keeps me sane
inside my chest

When the sun forgets to rise
I open the door
between my ribs
pull out a drawer
lift out a book
a dream
a video
mozart's genius
a memory
love in a Magaliesberg stream
imperfect bodies made perfect by desire
a silly joke
muddy hands
orange carrots in the earth

I pull one out
imprint it on my hameoglobin
feel it run through my body
like caffeine   whisky
sunshine
love

Against the Skin-Grey Bark

Against the skin-grey bark an orchid's petals
soft like an infant's folded hand
passionate as sex
wait for rain

....troepie shoots teenage bride....

Against the scrofulous trunk an orchid
soft as an infant's folded hand
dry as fear
wilts in the drought

....soldier dies in shooting accident....

Under the parchment leaves an orchid
soft like an infant's folded hand
alone as a mother
waits for tears
that no longer heal the scoured dongas
where brittle grass falls like people
into a crumbling grave

....child shoots himself with father's pistol....

Amongst the bone-grey roots an orchid blossom
soft like an infant's folded hand
broken as trust
shrivels in the machine-gun sun

Untitled

To find the way forward is the difficulty
to see through the smoke of burning women
past clouds of teargas   and dust
from running feet
to peer past the screen of tears
and aubergine walls of pain

is there a path
perhaps marked by long-forgotten hieroglyphs
perhaps untravelled   uncharted?
if I had eyes   like a spider
I might have enough to see

The Taste of Cabbage Keeps Me Sane

I dream of a common language
of a time when yes will mean
the same   to you and me
and perhaps will mean
let's think on it
and find a way together

I dream of saying no
and knowing
that's what you hear
I dream of hearing here
and knowing our borders
are the same

though I've drawn mine
in blue
and you in green

But when I wake
I find our words   broken
like swallows' wings
under cats' claws
and my tongue swells
like a loofah inside my mouth

I dream of spelling out
the simple truth
that must make hearts break
minds crack open
but when I turn the page
I find   we've grown old
illiterate   incontinent
with words

and I think I will grow
vegetables
wild   lustful of life
exotic   rotund with ripeness
that treacherous tongues can taste
but not pronounce

The Failure Of Imagination

I

On the grassy verge of suburbia
living there   but not a resident
while out walking
uncoiling the taut springs of his back
warped from weeding   and watering
a white fist met his black jaw
His day-dreams stumbled
knocked against white-painted walls
dog-high gates
the rhythm of kaffir-klapping rage
until there was too much blood
and his mind sprawled
lurching to the hot reality
of tar   and boots
swinging to meet ribs

He lay in the road like garbage
scattered by remorseless dogs
and his thoughts shivered like a mirage
in the desert of suburban gardens.

II

In the cold whip of winter
midday and mad
he burned his wife
turned her   among plastic plates
and sunlight soap
from dusky black   to pale
peeling like paint from an old door.

Her child cries for the breast
pink now like raw pork
and dreams of flames.

I rage with the pain
of everywoman   everychild
and phone an ambulance
and wait   with her
and the smell of charred flesh and paraffin
and the statement she might have made
melted like plastic onto her lips

I sing to her child
dark   like the skin she once wore
dark   like the tunnels of a father's soul
dark   like anger   like night
like sleep   and hot chocolate
soft   like hope   and milk
and I sing without words
sound without sense
to counteract the cold wail of human winter

Keith Gottschalk

Forbidden Dreams

Forbidden Dreams

tyres clawed halt on predawn tar,
rifle butts battered open the door;
they clumped down our passage in battledress
torchrays jabbed my eyes
baton prodded my shoulder,

i stirred   i mumbled

'man' they said
you're *dreaming* again?
under the riotous dreams amendment act
section 7
brrrrrackets bee e e e e e e e e e
I order your dream
loudly
in both official languages:
'DISPERSE FORTHWITH!'

Four poems from the Noodgedigte cycle.

siren howls. voice roars:
    AANDAG! *Attention*
    NOODTOESTAND! *State of Emergency*
& therefore: NOODGEDIGTE

[handwritten margin: need, want distress / danger / emergency] [State]

I Drie Hakies Een *[Brackets]*

Democracy is a country
where, when you hear a knock
at the front door at 5 am,
you know it's only the milkman.
             — Anon

the door knocked.
yellow datsun, white golf.
5.00 am:
six armed milkmen
put me in the jug.

six valets with pistols
rifle my wardrobe.
six librarians with revolvers
bring order to my bookshelves.
six macho suitors
guns in their holsters
proposition me:

    'Noodregulasies —
    drie hakies een.
    come with me
    & see my hakies.'

2 Die Regters-President

this oom,
oupahoed, twinkle eyes,
sits on the bed with his ledger
       asks: 'have you been assaulted?
       have you any complaints?'

'i feel disorientated,
they took away my watch'

— 'There are regulations.'

'they refuse me any reading,
even s.50 detainees are allowed books'

— '*You* can't choose what section
you want to be detained under.'

'they gave me no reason for detention,
not even the interrogator accuses me of crimes'

— 'The police have their methods.'

INTERCOM: Gevangene Silvia Nkomani, kom na records

3 Disinterment

> *In Ancient Egypt, the embalmed had their vital*
> *organs removed and sealed in canopic jars placed*
> *beside the sarcophagus*

Suddenly the corridor clutters:
it's offisiere en onder-offisiere,
deciphering cardboard labels
on sarcophagus lids: M4/85;
unsealing; excavating:
indicating — *kom*.

Sealing & unsealing each steel lid
into corridor; antechamber; corridor; corner;
corridor; corner, Ontvangs:

it's a sports jacket with a camera.

'Stand together' he orders Gareth Rossiter and me.
Click! and it's catacombing back.
'Last time this meant —'
says Gareth.

Hours later a *sersant* snaps:
pack your things.
— Am I being released?
— *nod*.

Quick! Your oranges to prisoner-reverend;
your peanuts to prisoner-pastor.
fumbling; pack:
goodbye-goodluck.
Snapping onderoffisiere;
then steel lid corridor predynastic
steel lid antechamber old kingdom
steel lid corridor middle kingdom
corner steel lid new kingdom
catacomb corner graceo-roman.

It's Ontvangs again, now ont-vanging:
hands back your canopic jars;
gives you heart; puts guts into you.

So, disinterred.
(will-they-recall-us?)

Numb, you stand outside a strange house
that looks like where you used to live.
All feels dirty, intruded upon;
you feel alien: a thing outside yourself.

4 Solitary Confinement: The Aftermath

Insomnia is:
— the inside light you can't switch off;
the forced night shift with no pay;
the *bewaarder* mugging your sleep.

— streetlight outflanking the curtain;
barking dogs, slamming car doors,
cop sirens, the bed empty beside you,
& aching eyeballs, too red to read.

— jolting awake, sweating
those nights after they retrenched you;
the weeks you suddenly awoke at 4 am
hearing a knock that wasn't
not hearing a knock that wasn't
after the knock that was.

— 4.15 am: first train. birdcalls.
      & bouncing between cloud & horizon,
      nightwatchman of the rocks,
      kaddish of the foghorn.

— groggy mornings;
stickiness that won't wash off;
boozeless hangovers;
getting your act together
when the day's leaving without you.

Pogrom: 18 May 1986

Terror floating in the air, terror
Against the wall in darkness hiding,
Terror through the silence sliding.
          — Chaim Bialik: *The City of Slaughter*

The City is unseeing; and has myriad eyes.

The City is friendless; and has innumerable friends.

The City is inhabited; bodies lie in its streets.

Yesterday Kishinev; today Nyanga Bush.

Yesterday the Black Hundreds; today Witdoeks.

Yesterday Jews; today our comrades.

They are displeased. They act.

Law grows out of barrels of guns,

death is a balaclava away.

We hurry, turn a corner;

our hopes & hiding places

one step ahead of them.

smoke ascends,

an epoch falls:

more than fire shall burn.

For Ashley Kriel Whom They Killed By Hazendal

A P.S. to Paton's 'To a Small Boy Who Died at Diepkloof Reformatory'

Modest opponent, leader of youth,
with every conception and comprehension
of the vast machinery set in motion
by your humble resistance
to the great forces of authority:
of Sub-Joint Management Centres,
Gikkoms, Komkoms and dockets,
principals, police, and verklikkers
kept moving, kept hunting by your defiance.

Our movement is moved to action by your dying:
when they handcuffed you, beat you,
threw you out the door face down,
shot you in the back —
the killing of a comrade means much work.

Then kommandant Creon says to *qabane* Antigone:

— *As long as I rule, you will not bury your brother.*

By uttering this command,
he made it our duty to bury our brother.

BISCO, CAYCO, UDF scramble:
soup, bread, cooking oil
for comrades coming to the wake;
posters, 200 000 pamphlets
distributed by sunrise at six stations;
donations, marshals, the vigil, the
bus collecting mourners leaving Cape Town;
so many details:
& lawyers briefed.

This day, and under a sky crying rain
Do we commit your body to the earth:
You, no longer child, now returned.

Of course they gas us,
try to seize our flag,
video the graveside crowds
so identikits can guide their hunters.
But the buffels, hippos, ratels,
circling, predatory, we defeated:

for we buried our brother.

After

At the burial of an epoch
no psalm is heard at the tomb.
— Anna Akhmatova: *In 1940*

After they detained the last woman
after they 'disappeared' the last activist
after they shot the last child

they grew afraid of the dead.

Throughout all graveyards of our land
they proclaim states of emergency:
they cordon off our dead with razor wire
they order roadblocks to stop wakes
they place our dead in solitary confinement
they forbid our dead visitors.
Should the dead rise
they decree summary execution.

They suspect: our dead are only pretending.

Their censers burn incense that burns eyes.
Their censors smash tombstones by night
ban inscriptions, wreaths & requiems.
Until, driven beyond endurance,
even our dead hold underground meetings
raise mounds of resistance
unearth alliances with the living:
guerilla a way to the light.

In our epoch the dead unite with the living.

The Police Museum In Pretoria
Compol Building, February 1976

in the Museum of Police
past the gallery of Handcuffs Through the Ages
through the hall of Tuxedos Worn by Police
                                    Commissioners
beyond the display of Whips & Canes

You can see:
the first police motor-bike
the first police dictaphone
the first criminal fingerprints
death-mask of hanged woman
suitcase of John Harris
wig of Braam Fischer
fractured skulls of murder victims
fingernails of arsonist
plastercast terrorist crawling out of hole
fallen policeman mourned by white cardboard horse
white-lace cuffed woman's hands
clasping Die Bybel Ons Vir Jou Zuid-Afrika.

it is rumoured
that if you whisper into the caretaker's ear
descend a secret staircase
unlock cobwebbed basement door

there
guarded by two police machinegunners in battledress
inside a large glass showcase
in a glass jar of formaldehyde
preserved for eternity

there
lies in state
the last successful writ
of *habeas corpus*.

from: *The True Believers' Prayer*
Matins: Preachers of the Left Bank

Our Hegemonic Power Bloc
Who art in conjuncture
Hallowed be Thy contradictions.
Thy Social Formation come,
Thy Mode of Production be done
In Praxis as it already is in Theory.
Give us this day our daily base
And forgive us our superstructure
As we never forgive those who deviate against us.
Lead us not into petty bourgeois utopianism,
But deliver us from false consciousness,
For Thou art the thesis, antithesis and synthesis,
Until classlessness.
Amen.

Crafting a Poem

always our searching:
mountains   buses
forests   schools
beaches   factories
examining & collecting *materiel*.

we size up: mass
                strength
                shape
                texture
& store them in cerebrum & cellar.

until the moment love pour into the mould
                rage   of
                laughter   the
                mourning   page.

so to work.
Hew a message. carve nuances of meaning.
chip against the grain of literary ideology.
retool orthography. sharpen calligraphy.

then, viewing: flashing eyelashes
                assonant voices
                gesturing hands
& always the cigarette smoke of friends
challenging, encouraging, warning.

next:	revisions, planing, polishing
now:	world *première*.
venue:	paintpeeled hall in ghetto.
air conditioning:	six smashed windowpanes.
interior décor:	wiremesh on windows
	flydirt on lightbulbs.
	newjacket on police informer.
audience preference:	less piano, more forte.

let your voice take command: plead, resonate, thunder.
they laugh, applaud, crowd round.
afterwards we put our words away
& walk back into the world.

Akhmatova Over Leningrad

the aluminium Tupolev trembles
slips across ice
then up, flees through frost, crystal,
crying to the sky.

inside reverberating fuselage,
racing over shrapnel & ice
evacuees flee famine, fatigue;
numbshocked sparrows darting on the wing.

in the streets, form snowdrifts, the dead spoke:
'we, the seven hundred thousand who cannot escape
entrust this symphony which can
written in hunger & lives.'

skeletal, cold
she sits in hand-me-down fur.
her palms
reverently bear:

Shostakovitch's Seventh	to feed orchestras	(forever)
dead husband	to feed firing squad	(once)
live son	to feed GULAG	(thrice)
worn ration cards	to feed herself	(always)

the sparrows fly to Tashkent
to the Uzbek nest
of the widow Nadezhda
pecking crumbs on Asia's windowsill
seven hundred thousand frozen in snow
mourn the Undead:
'we don't need your wreaths; go & lay them
on the living....'

½-Life Poem 02

wv — woman's voice
mv — man's voice
jc — jingle chorus

wv: The Dairy and Atomic Energy Boards
        bring you our state-of-the-art milk:
mv: ULTRA-KOEIBERG
        the only milk
        that gloooows
        as it floooows

wv: fortified with caesium 137!
           — alive with the exiting strontium 90 zing!

mv: Yes, top-of-the line ULTRA-KOEIBERG
           doesn't need pasteurising;
           it's auto-sterilising.

wv: ULTRA-KOEIBERG removes that unsightly hair
           on your arms and legs

mv: (it even removes unsightly arms and legs).

wv: You can enjoy a half-life today:
           just tear off the coupon printed on the lead foil
           & post in the reinforced concrete envelope
           to Chernobyl Dairies

mv: You need only buy one gramme!
           — we'll rush it to your front door
           in our disposable one tonne lead bottle.

wv: Arthur Murray says:
           Drink ULTRA-KOEIBERG
           and you'll click with every geiger-counter

mv: Dale Carnegie says:
           Men who drink Ultra-Koeiberg
           get much more
           out of their half-life

wv: and women who drink Ultra-Koeiberg
           are positively radiant!

jc: 50 million rontgens
           can't be wrong;
           after 28 years
           ULTRA-KOEIBERG's
           still half as strong!

Mount Nelson Hotel: 'Another Magical Big Band Evening, June 16, 1984'

'Sir — Madame — I have just the wine
for such a *special* occasion:
it's a dry red, robust, piquant;
quite an educated wine;
in fact, a cheeky impudent wine;
and it has body — 700, to be exact.
I must warn you, Sir, Madame,
that due to the unusual way it was, ah, processed,
its bouquet might make your eyes run tears.
But if you give it a free reign
it will match your class.

Cultivar:	Noir.
Estate:	Tiers.
Vintage:	Why, Sir, Madame, surely:
	it's the noble; late; harvest
	of 1976.'

Elegy to Challenger

For the seven astronauts killed 28 January 1986.

They vanished;
became sky;
a rain of metal tears
into the ocean.

Writhing, that cloud
became their cenotaph:
a wreath we laid
on our voyage to worlds.

Petition to My Interrogators

For Steve Biko & all killed in detention

When you come for me
two hours before dawn,
there will be no lightning or earthquakes,
nor even, in these busy times, an entry in the occurrences
diary.

but
it might cause some trouble.

Noooooooooo

i don't mean trouble with the *confession*.
i'm sure that can be fixed up in your usual businesslike
                                                            manner
— a few sleepless days & nights standing,
helpful coaching of fists, boots, electro-therapy
will tidy up any contradictory admissions (you can always
keep my cell light switched off to hold the power bill
                                                            down.)

so there will be no serious problems getting my signature
at the bottom of a blank affidavit form
or if you prefer, a voluntary self-written confession to
'High Treason'
        'skinny dipping'
                'eating my great-aunt'
                        'desecrating the sabbath'
                                'instigating the twentieth century,'

or whatever State Security requires that week.

no°°°°°°°°°°

that's not the trouble.
what I mean is: i don't want to inconvenience you
with the problem of garbage disposal

(i mean my post-mortem & inquest)

i could go on a hunger-strike
but the socialists know i'm a bit of a glutton,
so the underground would never swallow that one.

perhaps i could be found hanged in my cell
but the liberals know i'm atheist, awaiting no afterlife
so amnesty international would query another 'suicide'.

naturally i could always fall from a tenth-floor window
or down a staircase or two,
but my friends know i'm a member of the mountain club
so the press wouldn't buy it.

of course i could break my neck falling over a chair,
or hit my head against your office wall,
but my family always complained i was stiff-necked
& teachers all said i've got the thickest skull they'd seen,
so who would that convince?

if pressed i could try slip on a bar of soap,
but the jewish board of deputes is as frightfully touchy
about bars of soap as over tattooed lampshades.
so in these times of unexpected diplomatic alliances
Foreign Affairs would not consider that tactful.

last, i could attempt to die of a stroke
but my blood pressure normal, & being a blood donor
my doctor-father would never accept
                              such a death certificate.

so perhaps

(just to save all this inconvenience)
why not leave me alone ?

The Moon Is Coming
Cape Town 1980

the
          Moon
                    is
                              RISING

It is 0200hrs
when the Moon hits the dunes of Belhar
& the dune explode;
          shatter amber fire;
          bushes erupt flames.

PARAAT PARAAT PARAAT
10 AA Regiment fires tracer at the Moon;
the Minister of Justice bans all meetings;
Fatti & Moni's fire all striking workers;
the Riot Squad beats up Alexander Sinton High School;
armoured cars cordon off the dunes.

The Special Branch
think the Moon is the Committee of 81.
Fatti & Moni's
think the Moon is the Food & Canning Workers' Union.
Generaal Magnus Malan
thinks the Moon is Umkhonto we Sizwe.
The Moon says: *no comment*
The Moon only speaks to the people.

AANDAG AANDAG AANDAG
In their command bunker
total strategy is on the agenda.
Generaals & managing directors
posture; manipulate; threaten.
Generaal Constand Viljoen studies the map:
the workers study their paypackets.
On the map: the People's Republic of Angola.
In the paypackets:
poverty

          hunger
          NOTHING!

The *Generaal* smiles.

The workers don't smile.

From concrete wombs the *generaals* give birth: blitzkrieg

> napalm
>
> the armoured dash to Cela.

Out of our paypackets the workers give birth: union

> consumer boycott
>
> the strike for a living wage.

Police roadblock taxis;

poke submachine-guns under the seats,

but can't find the Moon.

Police dogs paw the dunes

but can't track the Moon.

30 Squadron chopper parabats to the dunes,

but can't kill the Moon.

Pretoria telexes:

> — detain Edna, Lila, Jakes
>
> BUT THE MOON HAS ESCAPED.
>
> & in burntout buses
>
> 3rd class train coaches
>
> inside factories
>
> chanting crescendos
>
> The
>
> > > Moon
> > >
> > > > Shall
> > > >
> > > > > Rise
> > > > >
> > > > > > Again!

How The Department of Cooperation And Development Rehoused Mrs Bhekeni Ngidi: 8 November 1977

An incident at Emalangeni, near Mpumalango, Natal

> under the sun
> the man.
>
> under the man,
> the bulldozer.
>
> under the bulldozer,
> the crushed pondok.
>
> under the pondok,
> the dead grandmother.
>
> under the grandmother,
> the rising people.

The Assassination of Jenny Curtis Schoon

> *your tasks live in us....*
> *you win our hearts, you become our banner....*
> *You live in those who continue the Revolution.*
> — Samora Machel: *Josina, you are Not Dead*

it was a whisper, trying not to be heard
    a shadow, trying not to be seen;
it was a day, when someone slipped away
    a night, when the dark moved

    it was war.

Jenny, NUSAS Vice-President,
runs NUSWEL, learns to drive,
tells workers their rights.
Jenny, IAS activist
drives herself hours beyond endurance
as I have never seen a human being driven:
— worker education by night
— union leaflets before dawn
— organizing throughout the day

then: marriage   (to Marius)
flight   (to Botswana)
underground   (for freedom)

sometimes, elsewhere
resistance appeared:
pylons, petrol dumps
dompas offices disappeared
& walls hung eyeless.

so, in Pretoria
parcels address themselves
to the problems of the day:
          Mnr Ongopotse Tiro, Gaborone.
          Mnr John Dube, Lusaka.
          Mev Ruth First, Maputo.
          Mev Jenny Schoon, Lubango.
all wrapped up,
all delivered.

she was our comrade
become statistic;
a ceremony when earth embraced;
— our anger
become the struggle.

Semiotic Events

> *...somewhere in the sugary*
> *hells of our seaports*
> *smothered by gases, an Indian*
> *fell in the morning:*
> *a body spun off, an anonymous*
> *chattel, some numeral tumbling,*
> *a branch with its death running out of it.*
> — Pablo Neruda: *The United Fruit Corporation*

We mobilise the alphabet into
strong syllables, crowded, chanting, fisted.
We deploy iambics, always rising —
we tense: transformative.

Somewhere, our city
stumbled under the blindfold of night.
Armed grammarians, unwarranted,
rupture a discourse:
— delete a parenthesis.
By the dawn rush-hour
only silent cartridges
lie dropped around like erasers.

Somewhere, scanned and stressed,
a frail phoneme, in solitary,
kicked to the floor:
a silent ending.

Continental Drift
Praise Poem For the People of Ocean View

IN THE BEGINNING
volcanoes, lava;
creative forces:
North America and Europe parted,
America drifted west,
Europe drifted east.
South America and Africa parted,
South drifted west,
Africa drifted east:

— 'that's the law of nature' they said.

Later, much later
lightning, earthquake;
destructive elements:
District Six razed, avalanched to Hanover Park.
Simonstown halved,
the amputated limb flung to Ocean View.

— 'Van Imoff's gift', they said

So descendants of Goringhaiqua and Gorachouqua
learnt that colonisers:
first, donate someone else's property as a 'gift';
second, demand you believe schoolbooks
that tell you 86% of South Africa
sommer fell off the back of a lorry.

— 'that's the law of history' they said.

Suddenly Fire!
                        Flood! Winds of change!
                        transformative forces:
                        streets crowds movement
                        days of burning barricades
nights of detentions, 'disappearances'.
Change, tectonic convulsion:
North America and Europe come together,
South America and Africa start uniting,
Crawford moves back to Claremont:
Ocean View shall return to Simonstown.

— 'that's people's power' we said.

Praise Poem of
The African National Congress

They have been through fire and steel, they have
conversed with stones
          — Yannis Ritsos: *Romiosyne*

I

Our shouts are peaks in a range of voices;
Our hands shape power in streets of strength;
Our comrades are a million men and women.

For twenty-six years they lived
entombed alive.
They conversed with stones
and the chains that shackled them
shackled thirty million of us.
They walked through the furnace,
they measured distance by roadblock,
and time by *section twenty-nine*.

their names:	comrade organiser
	comrade delegate
	comrade rank and file
their address:	underground, somewhere.
	Pollsmoor, Victor Verster.
their meals:	tension & cigarettes
their personal lives:	minutes between committees
	& agenda
their love-making:	under matters arising
their destiny:	death
	— and our liberation.

II
the new tsars ride by helicopter
the arrogant arm points:
'Kruispad, Khayalitsha —
van daar tot daar....'

& and it is done.

this epoch's cossacks
ride hippos, buffels,
use guns not swords
gas not knouts;
the whips remain whips.
& in Langa, KwaThema, Mamelodi
upon the dust of our roads
red blotches become our shrouds.

Our ghettos are loaded into lorries:
beds, pots, corrugated iron;
exiled by warlords,
banished to Babylon.
For the hands that shape metal,
steer machines,
for daily commuters of the abyss
who hew gold four kilometres down
suffocating in the inferno;
for our workers:
— the compound
— the firings
— the 'disappearance'.

Our comrades travel door upon door,
defying fear & fatigue;
strengthening people,
building organisation:
— COSAW
— COSATU
— ANC

& when they are seized
by the SADF Civilian Cooperation Bureau
— Siphiwo Mtimkulu, Mathew Goniwe,
Griffith & Victoria Mxenge —
their bodies lie 'cooperated'
through the streets of our land.

III
Ah! Madiba!
Izwi labantu!
Ikhakha lenkhululeko!
Umkhonto weSizwe!

Wazalwa uyinkosana, wena wajika wangabantu
Mfundi, ungumfundisi wetitshala zakho
Lutsha, ungumququzeleli weenkonde
Mphathi, wamatshantliziyo awuluthobelanga ucalu-calulo
Mlandeli wecharter, wazibhengeza ezi nkululuko
Mmangalelwa, utyholwa ngokungcatsha isizwe osithandayo
Mguquli wamajele, wakway' amazambane
Mhambi, uyityhutyhil' iAfrika
Msebenzi mgodini, urhubuluze phantsi komhlaba
Gqwetha, usilwele isizwe
Mmangalelwa, uwuphakamisile umthetho
Banjwa, umbambile urhulumente.

mayibuye!   audience: iAfrika!
masibuye!
makabuye:
Nelson Rolihlala ManDEEEEEEla!
Rolihlala AmaaaaaaaaaaanDEla!
AMAAAAAAAAAAAAAAAAAANDELA!
ncincilili.

Praise Poem of the
Congress of South African Trade Unions

They fear a 80-year old comrade
they fear a comrade without a leg
they fear comrade Oscar Mpetha
they fear com Ray Alexander
they fear com Liz Abrahams
even dead they fear com Rev Marawu
even dead, they fear com Neil Aggett
even dead, they fear Andries Raditshela.

They shackled us with bantu amendment laws
now they try labour relation laws:
'you are not fired — you are rationalized.'
'you are not fired — you are freed from your contract.'
'you are not fired — you are deregulated.'
'you are not fired — you are privatised.'
'you are not fired — you dismissed yourself by striking.'

By the UIF gebou we sat down & wept.
You are no longer a man but manlike —
'MANLIKE A TOT L on 40%:
Come on time! Siiiit quiet!
Producccccce your identity!
Kom! Teken! Voeeeerrtsak!'

They fear the working class; they fear COSATU,
they steal our GST to print their *Trade Union Titbits*;
they call our shop stewards, Sedition, Hoofverraad,
they detain our union activists, they bombed
                              COSATU House
Their mellow yellow sits in the sky, pretends to be god;
it fears Elijah & Moses speak the truth.

Comrades Elijah & Jay say:
ORGANISE!
Build our unions!
Build COSATU locals!
Build the revolutionary alliance COSATU-ANC-SACP!

'AANDAG!
       NADEMAAL dit na my blyk,
       Dat omstandighede ontstaan,
       Kragtens die byvoegheid aan my verleen,
       By artikel twee sit-in-hakies een sluit-hakies,
       Verklaar ek derhalwe hierby,
       Dat ek 'n noodtoestand toewy.
       Gegee onder my Hand en die Seël van die Republiek,

              I beg to remain,
                     Your obedient servant,

PW FW Magnus Kobus Adriaan Assocom FCI
Chamber of Mines. Punt. Volgende reel.'

'KUYA KUBAKHO umsebenzi nokhuselo!
Bonke abasebenzayo bayakukhuleka ukuseka
                                amaqumrhu ezorhwebo,
ukonyula abaphati babo nokwenza
izivumelwano ngemivuzo nabaqeshi babo.

THERE SHALL be work & security!
All who work shall be free to form trade unions
to elect their officers & to make wage agreements.

ABANTU bayakuxhamala ubutyebi belizwe!
Ubutyebi belizwe lethu,
ilifa lomntu wonke wase Mzantsi Afrika,
bayakububuyiselwa ebantwini.

THE PEOPLE shall share in the country's wealth!
The national wealth of our country, the heritage
of all South Africans, shall be restored to the people.

VIIIIIIIIIIIIIVA the birth of SACTWU!
VIIIIIIIIIIIIVA the unity in SACCAWU!
FAWU —   grow stroooooong!
SADWU —   grow stroooooong!
SARWHU —   grow stroooooong!
T&G —   grow stroooooong!
Phantsi   ngeLabour Relations Law!
Phambili   ngeliving wage!
PHAMBIIILI ngesocialism!
Amaaaandla kubazenbenzi!
AMAANDLA kuCOSATU!
ncincilili.

Awareness Programme:
The Grammar Lesson

Class
      always
we have had prose.

mood: imperative
case: possessive
tense: pluperfect
voice: passive, negative
person: singular

examples: 'moenie'
                  'toonbank gesluit'
                  'slegs blankes'
                  'waar's jou pas?'
                  'laat die donner vrek'

this is called: traditional grammar.

Class
      for today & for tomorrow
let's poem.

mood: indicative
case: accusative
tense: the future
voice: active & positive
person: collective

examples: forbidden couplets cuddle

                students quatrains boycott

                dactyls distribute leaflets

                iambic & trochaic feet

                          march to secret rendezvous

                                with vigilant anapests.

clandestine poems scatter leaflets

worker poems strike for wages

militant poems barricade streets

cadre poems coordinate rhythms

armed poems

slip across patrolling frontiers

through nights without passes

dig caesuras to trap statutes

ambush convoys of detention warrants

fire rocket-propelled stanzas at SASOLs;

people's poems

mass in raised fist cantos

chant the Charter, sing *Umzima Lomthwalo* —

This, class

        we call:

                transformational grammar.

Musee Des Mauvais Arts: Grabouw Police Station, April 1980

For the Kromco apple strikers who were victims of electric torture
       (Following W H Auden)

About suffering they were never wrong.
Luitenant Marius Retief tied wires
around their little fingers,
stood the strikers barefooted on electrodes
('it looked like a phone with handle & wires'
the youthful victims recalled)
You will climb the wall until you confess,
bragged the interrogators.
Six teenage apple packers,
electric burn scabs on their fingers, never forgot:
while their dreadful martyrdom ran its course
the Elgin apple gentry cultivated old strains of roses
groused into whisky & soda
& pleasured the hunt.

In the Deciduous Fruit Board poster, for instance,
apples glow-green, dew-dappled, sylvan:
shine their vitamin innocence, packaged arcadia.
While Kromco apple packery shareholders
cash their fat-fleshed dividend cheques, their
teenage beachbuggy kids, who must have heard
                                  something amazing,
teenagers screaming in the police station,
chewed gum, finished the demi-john,
checked a far-out tube to shoot , & jorled off.

Unbelievable Fairytales For Children

The First Tale

One summer morning, Comrade Metternich, Prince Pol Pot I, and the Right Honourable Dr Verwoerd were drinking coffee in the conservatory.

They discussed the eternal paradox:

Why did people never appreciate what was for their own good? When they spoke these words, the leaves rustled nervously on the branches.

The Second Tale

After one lunch in autumn, Comrade Nebuchadnezzar, His Majesty Joseph Stalin I, and the Honourable Piet Koornhof were taking Van der Hum in the smoking room.

They discussed another eternal paradox:

Millions dreamt of travelling to far-off places. Why then, when granted this at the ruler's expense, did they so desperately resist?

As they spoke these words, all the leaves fled from the trees.

Morakabe Seakhoa

Future Tense

Mantoa (03.07.1986)

News of your coming
was cool water for
A man long in the desert.
Like new clothes in the eyes
Of a child.

Excitement hung long
Like sweet perfume that
Many washes fail to drive away.
Oh, the news was like peppermint
On my palate—
Soothing and tingling as the soft
Soft melody of a piano.

Reading and re-reading your letter
Brought you so near.
Impatience reigned
Hours became days,
Years, even!

In this momentary blissful
Stupor,
In this happy weightlessness.
A jailor shouted my name.
I responded and rushed,
Prancing like a foal on
The morning dew.

A telegram he handed me:
'Your sister passed away yesterday'
Instant darkness fell all around me,
Gloom replaced (that) joy.
My ears were shut to what he
Further said.

I hobbled to my cell
With sagged shoulders
Like a rain-soaked hen.
Is it true? Can it really be true?

Oh my sister, my dear, dear sister.
You who but just yesterday
Promised to come,
You, who, only a day
Remained for us to meet
Dearest, sweetest sister.

Our Epitome

Once, you were a leader
Many times (before), your voice
was that of us all
You were our hearts and our eyes
You were lionised by old and young;
Countryman and foreigner,

Once, you were us.

Now, you are like a wounded lion:
Your limpy and unsure walk

Is that of a horse ravaged by wild dogs,
Your once-brave face filled with grimaces of
pain below the seemingly happy surface

Not many of us now hanker
for your voice anymore
Few among us remember the good you did;
Our memories of you are that of
long-forgotten dinosaurs;
Posterity's knowledge of you will be like a
once-rich garden unplouged for centuries.

Comrade Darkie

After all the death-bells have tolled,
After all the screams and faintings of sorrow
Have ravaged our souls,
After all the shocks and wailings
Have quietened,
The reality of your departure
Still seems a bad sad dream
To be quickly dismissed and forgotten.

To us the reality is seeing you
Running the length and breadth
Of the Modder Bee playing field,
To us the reality is seeing you
Struggling for freedom
And People's Education for all.
Of you chairing our meetings
In times of crisis,

Walking in that style
That reflected the fighting
Spirit of youth:
A true mirror of the Young Lion.

In you we have lost a soldier,
Killed like a soldier in action.
Among us a gap has opened,
But as we say and sing:
ANGEKE SIWULAHLE UMKHONTO WE SIZWE.

Your place shall be filled
By many more of your calibre

It is hard to think of you
In the past tense,
To think of you as dead
Is real hard.
We still think of you a
Freedom lover and fighter;
A young lion
A patriot hammering together
Our divided land,
A combatant for People's Power,
A revolutionary to the end!
Victory or death!
We shall over come!
HAMBAKAHLE QHAWE LAMAQHAWE!

Thirteen Year Old Siphiwe

I listen to him daily as his
Youthful mind forever gives
Off sparks of wisdom
Taught to him by the hard
Life of prison and apartheid,
This young one whose place
Is surely in a school room
But now a prison cell
Is his class room and home,
His teachers the oppressive
Situation and the sharing of ideas with
Other comrades.

All he understands and knows
He bares to all around him,
All he does not understand
He asks all around him
Always ready to accept
Corrections that are building,
Never tiring to reject and correct
Those that are misleading and destroying.

Like a magnet, nothing escapes his interest,
Holding to it like it was the only
Thing existing,
He never gets enough,
Knowledge to him is food.

Thinking of how young he is,
You realise crime is here committed!
This glittering wisdom is laid to waste
By the rulers who fear in it
The dynamite ready to explode
This myth of white supremacy
And class bondage and domination.

In Solitary Confinement

The day shuffles lazily along;
Seeming to stop whenever you think
When comes tomorrow,
Or when is the day of release.

Like a disturbed tortoise, the sun
Sits nailed up there motionless
Staring down intently as if
Taking interest and pity on you.

Sunrise you never see,
Only an officer with a well-rehearsed
'Alles reg!?' tumbling from his lips.
Your watch is the sun's rays
Stroking the tall jail walls
You badly miss the crimson setting sun.

With nothing in your hands to
Hasten the day on,
With no book nor paper to shut out
The stench of boredom and aloneness,
You think, think, think till your nerves
Are like over-stretched guitar strings.

Days pass,
Weeks melt into months.
When am I going home?
No one tells, no one seems to know;
After the troubles are over, some say.
Hell am I a prisoner of war?

The mind takes wings to freedom,
Free as a bird it flies across seas and mountains
Visiting lands free and friendly,
Rejoicing and mingling with people merry and unfettered,
Soaring high the mind goes,
Taking me to the warring streets of our bleeding land
Where People's Democracy is hammered out.

Come night, my bosom friend!
In you I take pleasure,
Bring those sweet dreams once again!
Let them caress me till the sun is up!
Oh, night!
My all-comfortable plane!
Fly me fast to the day of my liberty!

Mother

Ma, dear, cry not when you learn
I'm detained again;
Lose no hope if I'm to serve years
In jail again.

Keep strong, gain strength
Even when the hangman's noose

Tightens around my neck.
My blood will hasten the end
Of man's brutality to man,
The flow of my blood will
Be the stream of water
At the root of the tree of liberty.

Let no insult hurt you, Ma,
Let all insinuations and
Words of despair strengthen your heart.
Don't drown in self-pity,
Allow yourself not to be pitied;
Feel no shame, heed no disgrace.
Take them all in your stride
like all those months I was in your womb.

Courage, dear Ma, take courage.
Take pride in me,
My, our trials, our tribulations
Are not in vain,
ours is a worthy cause,
A noble cause to end all suffering, all bondage.
To bring peace, harmony and comfort.

No war is without casualties, Ma.
We are children of the war,
Moreover, we are soldiers,
We must fight to the bitter end,
Until the day of victory,
Until we have won our liberty!

Parents

We are your children
Who but just yesterday were babes
Crying on your laps,
Who hid shyly behind your skirts
From slightest danger or stranger;
Who clung to you for protection
Away from the assuring fires of home.

Yes, it is your children
Who are mercilessly dragged
Into the rigours of manhood and womanhood
Before we are teenagers;
Whose blood is splattered across
The streets of our land;
Whose blood continue to drip
From the hangman's gallows.

We are your children!
We are the products of the
Situation.
Shaped and moulded
By the march and demands of our time.
We are the resisting and fighting
Victims of circumstances
We aim to transform.

We cry no more.
We fear no more.
The agony of shock and pain steels
Our determination even more.
Death we face square,
Death is part of the process.

No longer do we cry 'Senzenina'
For now we know the cancer
Ripping our society apart.
Our crime is our dream and fight
For a free tomorrow,
Of South Africa knocking heavily
On the door of man's brotherhood
To man.
For South Africa free and non-racial,
Where there'll be no rich idlers
And hungry toilers.

We are your children
Unceasingly and untiringly
Marching on to a People's future;
We have reached the point of no return.
Ever forward, Never backward!
The future is now in our hands,
The future is us!

Joblessness

Driven from never-warming
Tattered blankets
Haunted by hungry squeals
Of my children
Angry rumblings gnawing my
Stomach like a pack of hungry
Wolves,
Pained by the fast-aging face of my
Young Wife:
I stand accused in the world of
Planned unemployment,
Of deliberate and artificial
wretchedness.

I brave chilly winds of winter
mornings,
Calling at ports I never
Knew before,
Tossed hither and thither by
Gleams of rumoured hopes
And promises,
Often sleeping in dark alleys
And prison cells like a
long lost masterless dog,
A vagabond forever a loser
In the jungle law of the rich
And the mighty,
Always a victim in the unequal
struggle between labour and capital....

With cap in hand I bow
Cowed before men of capital
And influence,
Catching any penny, any morsel
Thrown my way, swallowing
Any pride threatening to
Swallow me.

I call men of power and
Riches all by titles revered
(Deserving and undeserving alike)
Stooping to lowness I
never before thought Human.
Choices are not mine:
The realities of my station
In life.

New Order

The old order is screaming
With unceasing pangs of child birth
The old rulers run in vain with
Remedies to calm her down,
But the new child comes kicking,
Kicking, kicking out of the old

useless womb

The new order is born.
The old order is gone;
Dead and forgotten just
Like the dreaded snake
After child birth

Life and Living

The agony and adversity of life
Is like a needle between finger
And nail thrust
Like sudden blindness has come:
Heavens seem to be falling down
On you,
Horizons close in on you
Like angry tides of a turbulent sea.
The very foundations of the earth
Crumble and dissolve from under your feet.
You feel you're sinking down a dark and endless pit:
Confusion becomes an absolute certainty
And death seems to be an imminent infinity
From which there appears to be no sanctuary.

In life's times of sorrow and pain
To cry or not to cry drive no pain away.
To laugh or not to laugh
Brings nearer
No joy nor solution,
The answer to all life's ebbs and flows,
To all joy and ecstasy
Resides in understanding
Understand(ing) why things
Happen the way they do,
Why we are here
And not anywhere else.
Why not yesterday or the coming day
But today!

Why it had to be you
And not anyone else.

Understanding!
Understanding is the key
To the webs and dark hidden
Secrets entangled into the essence
Of life and the world.

Life is about turning disadvantages
Into advantages:
Turn your enemy's
Sword against his belly.

Life is the business of arriving, seeing
And conquering.
Of ever learning, ever acclimatising
And ever winning,
Of always being sensitive and responsive
To the new and ever-changing
Conditions of life.

This has been the mark of humans
Since the beginning:
To act otherwise is to slide down
The path of defeat and death.
Following in the footsteps of dinosaurs
That lie buried in the ashes of oblivion!

Turn disadvantages into advantages,
Let the discomforts of exile
Be your armoury for our happy future.
Flatten the walls of oppression and
Inhumanity dividing the free world
From our land of bondage.
Transplant that tree of liberty
To our weeping soil.

Turn disadvantages into advantages.
Turn the prison walls
Into schools oozing with the
Bright vision of a happy tomorrow.
These dehumanization and degradation cesspits:
Let them become academies of liberation.

This is the river where warriors
Receive their baptism
This is the well from which
Democrats and patriots
Sip waters of liberation,
Where new men and women are born.

Let's take our rigs and drill.
Let's take as much water for the future.
For the desert is outside
It takes time and energy
To find an oasis.

Let's eat and drink enough,
Take and grasp enough
To share and shed light
on the correct path
So that the horizons of people's
Victory may be nearer and clearer.
And the road away from tyranny
To people's rule may be easy.

Some Lessons

A runner wishing to make the distance
Starts off slow and small,
Increasing speed apace with what the distance takes,
He reaches the winning line with the ease of a stroller.

A runner wishing to make the distance does not sprint
from the word go.

He has nothing in common with a gluttonous cow:
Biting more than can be chewed only ends in
constipation.

So, take it easy:
We all have to bend in order to jump,
We all chafed our knees before we stood up and walked.

Ari Sitas

Songs, Shoeshine & Piano

These lyrics try and combine four basic musical traditions —
and more specifically the relationship between words and
rhythms that we find there: jazz, maskanda, sailors' ballads,
and ragas. I hope that they, together with the more
conventional statement thrown in here and there, make
sense.

My gratitude has to go to a great number of musicians and
oral poets, whose help in discussing music, rhythm and
language shaped many of these words and their 'patterning'.

Finally, many thanks to the Culture and Working Life gang
who convinced me to continue jotting ditties and, insisting
that all this was more comprehensible than my usual
nonsense.

My soccerite friends must not laugh at the choice of title:
Screamer Shabalala has taken the phrase from musical
performing traditions to describe his own physical
compositions. I am taking it back: to describe the physical
torment that performs us.

Ari Sitas, 1991

I. The Journey

We yanked our sail over the pole against our breath
for an inward journey

There is a hole in our heart somewhere where cancers
grow and pulse
and counterflow

and so we descended

searching for that, and for the navigating constellations
that must be there
in that murk

in the springs of dreamtime

in the passages where death, naked and lashed,
rows
people to ether

We found after the first totems, the lung, the heart, the
liver, the lawn, the familiar rolling hill, the slope over
and into the makhopokopo landscape

and the shanties were spread out as far as the heart
                                                  could feel
until they became the known world

these shacks, this time were not to burn
and even if you lit them up they did return to spook you

the breath calmed,
the sails folded
and many voices howled,
rhythmed and moaned
in the known world
the shanties were spread out as far
as the heart could fathom,
rhythm or counterflow
we moored our craft
in this new world of pulse, of cinder.

II. Shrieks

Our thoughts speed-by the cracks of the fierce wind
and the waves crashing the stern
scrambling our brains
they speed-by the timber-furrows left open by Dias
to rest at the place where the half-slave knelt
where the half-slave cried about his karma
in the place of the monkey, the serpent, the gun

the place where the baas plays lambkin come unto me
the place of the mixed-root
of the babble of scripture
and Allah and Jesus and Krishna
and hallellujah the abalozi are not coming home
marking the start of the difacane of the brain

and our thoughts are broken
by the shriek of the night-bat
the fruit-bat
and the high shriek of the woman
whose gut is displayed on the tip of spears

our thoughts are broken
in this dump
in this marvellous dump

past the cracks of the fierce wind

we were caught sailing home

'S'pume Topiya
Sihamba ngomoya
Thina solala
Emakhaya'

III. Shantytown

At the squatter camp the shanties
do not leave space to plant a universal something
they just brag of these items hammered together
and joined and piled up

and he who packs the dagga-pipe there
he gave me the biscuit tin he had salvaged
before they pulped it at the dump
I love him for that
and I use it for a seat

Durban is pretty when it doesn't rain
and when the river doesn't swell
the shanties sparkle from afar
and there is
no
loss,
of hope.

These shelves, they are the best
I got them with the bricks
from Ghandi's settlement
before the bluflies stole them for themselves.

IV. Shantytown

The earth has crusted hard
and all thousand little feelings
have stiffened into structures
ejaculations, harsh, distinct
without form, crude, scattered eyesores
each one a little economy of hunger
each one loud, aggressive
this space is singularly mine
my rags this side
that side, thine.

Stiff tips press down the chords
my right thumb pulls a string
my fingers pluck my echo chambers loud
hat skewes the eyesights
lids tick off flies

that sun squeezes out my cheeks until they water
neck strains so you can trace the words
they travel up the windpipes to the skies
this space is singularly mine
my rags this side
that side, thine.

This song has hardened like a hide
like our collective skin
stretched out for you to drum onto it a stick of fury
stretched over like a tent to stop and catch the rain
softened at night to tremble with these simple hearts
with sighs,
to feel the scraping of that corrugated tin
this song has strained its patience to its tether
cardboard, asbestos guttering and twine
my rags this side
on that side, thine.

V. Contract

I did not chose to have to work so early it was so much
easier stalking the shops and playing soccer from the
pylon to the fat neighbour's fence
But as the school pants faded from the kickdives and the
roughage of stone
I boarded the bus: yawning
and in winter when it was still dark and when we were
still huddled up, there was that hooligan moon lighting
our cheekbone blinking farewell — you traitor's carcass

A piece of metal, steel, almost square I had to file to shine
its edges cut and smooth and slant
and a hole square with grooves I had to centre
and I sweated anxious because in every four three of
them were wrong
and the pressure
and I goggled and goggleyed and centred
until I centred more
and my fingers were hewn with iron filings
I smiled and showed and smiled lookhear I'm good
forsure
I loveme
I make forty-five edges cut and smooth and slant and
centred
but the hooligan moon with its falsetto voice
and its guitars, disturbs my nightshifts still.

VI. Howling at the Moon

Leave your shantytown ghetto face faces long and ugly
Everyday from work light a fuse and blow
leave your troubles in the kitchen and the factory
follow me
     past the roadblock and the torchlight
     let the rhythm jerk and roll

Heita, ride with me and my guitar as I tapdance on a
moonbeam on my rocket to the stars
Yes, ride with me and my guitar as I tapdance on my
rocket to the stars

— You said I was wrong or I was right, you said and said
come on you must be joking; responsibility; uhlonipha is
the name of the game; but, I said and said till I was
howling that no I am different, I am good, I have done
good, I have done well, I have a shirt. Here I have a shirt
to prove that I have been to school and as you are
wrong or am I wrong, I do not know you said and said
that I was wrong and I said and said till I was howling
that I

am useless
come on leave your worries and come
ride with me and my guitar as I tapdance on my rocket
to the stars.

And the pinkdressed whoopers sing, they flap and echo
      from below
      satellite transmitted
      to and fro:

'Cause we live
in ghettoland
in sour-milk-and-honey-land
the brand that earns no kruggerand
cause we live...
cause we live in ghettoland
in goldmine and in compoundland
in shackland and in pianoland
cause we live in
JAZZLAND
cause we live in
JAZZLAND
dancing black and blue'

Leave your shantytown ghetto face faces long and ugly
Everyday from work light a fuse and blow
Leave your troubles in the kitchen kitchen and the
factory
follow me
past the roadblock and the torchlight
let the rhythms jerk and roll.

— Is that a moan I hear or is it a howl, like all howls
people go howling at the moon and screech their blues
away, or is it something else a siren perhaps, tearing
each hour to shreds or is it a dog yearning for
something, a romantic dog searching and searching or is
it me suffering and tearing my lungs out howling at my
life...I've been to school, you've been to school, I am
soweto '76 and cool

Heita, ride with me and my guitar as I tapdance on a
moonbeam on my rocket to the stars.

VII. Worker of the Word

I write, I am a writer
I write because they said I was not a writer
I write because they said
I was not good enough to be a writer
I write because they said the only good thing for me was
to be a good machinist,
or a clerk or something sideways
I write because they said I had no talent
I write because they said I was a nobody
that my father was a miner
and my mother was a bore
and my brother had a tattoo of sealife on his shoulder

I write and say here I am
here are we
we are one
and an injury to all
is an injury to me.

VIII. Blues

We've been told we are nothings, we know, by the
people who know how to judge in just proportions
We did never think to find treasure in the deeper
meanings and clues god stacks for our kind
We could never feel the solemn strain or the
melancholy note from a landscape of city, bed or moon
We've been told we are nothings, we know, by the
people who stake many claims in this workshop of
wonders

> We're good for, good-for-nothing-goodfors
> good enough for shoeshine and piano that's true
> shoeshine and piano and blue

Dear, we are of the ugly sort the kind that wore ill-
fitting suits and dresses in the sixties
the type that couldn't cut the type
thickset and coarse with square features
and when we wore a shiny thing it always was too shiny
— bad genes from father's too much ahootching and
aswaying home
and mother's vericose creepers up her skirt —
But this is not the stuff for ballads
these moans, dear,
do not belong to this prancing shanty town

Our mold was not cut and poured
for those creatures' notice
who wear their legs and snouts
until they make you tingle
and make you curse your stunt, your sheen,
your life, that's true, shoeshine and piano
and blue.

IX. Crooning

We hurt from the lives we will never live, those better
lives, those lives ELSEWHERE
We go dying each day a little bit more, drunk from the
shame we inhale
flattened here, we go dreaming of invisible lungs balloon-
pump-upping our threadbare skins
we go spooning-in here the filth of this city, meekly
smiling and escaping too soon into the alleys

> to croon
>> we go crooning:
>> sink into the hour, the twilight hour
>> devour the night
>> guydoll, jellyroll your spite away

Father worked across the bay where they used to cut
blubber and meatpacks from whales
I swear to his last his hands sweated-out codliver oil and
on his last our lives started sinking
and me, his little ground-sailor with my Sunday blue and
white collar and hat entered the fishlife
the payroll of bones, the hurt of the other side, the
wrong side the crusted beard salt-life apprenticed

to croon
>we go crooning:
>sink into the hour, the twilight hour
>devour the night
>guydoll, jellyroll your spite away

I weep for the mermaid, tattooed or eaten added tuna
and parsley or admired on the porthole's mouth
We hope as we moan, as we stir in the murk, in the
voodoo rites of factory pots and pans and molasses
we despair of the lies of the other life and tear open all
angels reading their innards for signs
we snap-off their wings and we start flapping and pacing
about incanting our lost years and speed-off

to croon
>we go crooning:
>sink into the hour, the twilight hour
>devour the night
>guydoll, jellyroll your spite away

We hurt from the lives we will never live, those better
lives, those lives ELSEWHERE

X. Pantsula Brains

Down the street we go
down the street we go
with our hands in your pockets
we go
with our pantsula brains revving high

We've got to leave this city, this city is dying
they are shutting down the docks
We've got to leave this city, the girls don't swing
don't dance they just sing them
Brenda Fassie tunes

Down the street we go
with our hands in your pockets
we go
off and about we tear
with our pantsula brains revving high

We've got to leave this city, they are cutting
cutting the maqabane down
we've got to leave it, they are searching
for abathakhathi day and night

Let's go to the land where the dreams have rested
Let's go to the place where we are not for hire
stoke a different fire
with our pantsula brains revving

singing to go
itching to fly
loving to stay

XI. Mango Tango

We used to dance the toyi-toyi
but then from France there came 'tua tua'
and from then came tropical fruit from joburg
some people there do the guava juice
'quattah'!
we here, we do the mango...tango

after the grinding day
i strut out
marching a two-step, leap, a two-step, leap and block
groaning about
and then I tap my sole, tap my soul,
and spring a two-step, leap, a two-step, leap we go.

i am dancing look twisting to the end of time
i am dancing look this road is mine
i am blasting till the walls of Jericho fall
i am dancing past verwoerd, voster, botha their friends
and all

i am leaping look i am the egret shooting thru the sky
i am the eland
the hippo
i am the casspir-catcher fly

i am water
i am the waterfall
the downpour
i am the spark of all
them gone and coming back to life

after the grinding day
i strut out
marching a two-step, leap, a two-step, leap and block
groaning about
and then I tap my sole, tap my soul,
and spring a two-step, leap, a two-step, leap and go.

we used to dance the toyi-toyi
but then from France there came 'tua-tua'
and from then on came tropical fruit from joburg
some people there do the guava juice
'quattah'!
we here we do the mango...tango.

XII. Waterfront

You are this leather in time
shine over the cracks, have a drink
lovecurse the moon
tonight is the night surely the night
to stalk the waterfront

                 and the saxophone bursts you away

You are this leather this time
edging-in past the first spring days
(whatever that means when you are facing this ocean)
forget how your skin cracked-up this winter and how
when it was rubbed
it flaked
it was sandpapered and shredded

And by now your fingers have the smooth feel
tapeasy, greaseasy feel
like an oily sheen, like you were used-to-sheen
when you smeared fish for the pan
By now you dream of her hair and you kiss
and you nightmare yourself silly
waking up with a hennaed tongue

        and the 'coonbands' strum for you

You are this leathered time
and deep down you know
that under the flannel and silk
and the coarse elastic that holds your shell
your imperfection
(my God how do You manufacture all the others)
deep down
craters exploded matter
roughed-up hide
along the trunk of your years
by now you walk past the flickering lights of their eyes
eyes that hurt
as your hooves are counter-tapping lamely
the rhythms of fears

        and the violins weep for you

Past these first springtimes
your times' leathers
tramp by the scents of ginandtonic, resin and tar
tramp by the scents of lubricants easing your joints
the lubricants and oils, your overhaul's not perfect

— of lower class, of lower ape
as the first hint of summer seeps through wet
through your starched shirt
By now you imagine the night which will once more
conjure the bands to rattle the floors

Conjure her too:
she is this leather
pinned
wind-flapping
on the coastline

    radiostations pray for you

XIII. Blood/Igazi

It is hard to be asked to grieve once more
    after every feeling was torn-out
    with every fingernail torn

it is hard to be asked to celebrate still
    when the pain still splits
    each heartbeat in two

it is hard to play the festival songs and share
    the season's first fruit
    when the reeds are scattered and broken

when the roots float up scratching at nothing

hard to be human
to laugh
but we must
we have learnt
we will try harder and laugh
all the way home
sihamba ngomoya
thina solala emakhaya

I shall bring the milibo
we shall share in our umkhosi wokweshwama
we shall shake the earth in our umgubho of light
lahla
lahl ucelemba

it is hard when our homes are broken
bafowethu
it is hard to smile when your face is frozen
into the frame of friends
who have flown out of windows
and those who shrink each day in the locker

Ithathe uybambe
the wind, inkhanyamba, pounding on the shacks
uybambe,
the waves splashing our fishing boats
uybambe
the devastation of fire in the workshops
uybambe
the rocks and stones we eat to line the stomach
uybambe
the hardship, the nightmare, the famine

but
search for the mzila back home
uybambe,
the reeds are waiting for their player
the shoes for the dance
the dead to come home
the moon, the dream, the bread,
isinkwa
are waiting to be brought home too.

lahla, lahl' ucelemba
siphuma topiya
sihamba ngomoya
thina solala
emakhaya

Mandela Rally, 1990

XIV. Dancing Shoes

Got these shoes through struggle
each godforsaken day
hid the bonus from my mother
lied about my pay
now they dance me
watch them twist
watch them break my bones
off to town for some romancin
going down in dancing shoes and dancin

Took them down to serve my contract
to dig down the hole
where the walls are singing
in my mvukuzane-role
now they dance me
and I lick them
with my tongue to shine
watch them break my bones
going down in dancing shoes and dancin

And I tap
and I tap-tap
like a Tap-tap Makhatini
yini mfo
like a tap-tap
near Inanda dam
and I tap
and I swoon
and they dance me
and they move me, tap-tap...home.

They've been swinging all my troubles
in this two-cent fokall strife
they've been turning my emotions
making meatball of my life
now they dance me
watch them twist
and turn
and twist
and burn the sole
and set my soul alight
there's no time now for romancin

going down West street
in my dancing shoes and dancin
with another three thousand prancing
chanting down the block.

XV. East Rand, Our Past

The past strikes at your sternum
and your plywood creaks at the joint
as your memory-ark gets
grounded tonight on the airwaves

You pray that also those friends are not dead
and you hope that they did not do some of the killing
as you hear that the Vosloorus hostels
are smouldering still
and your Zulu friends you left there
are not the ones who are skull collectors

Your past is conspiring against you
on this winter night

As you write the lines the dust at the union office
with its customary grime still scrapes your lung
and the names of the people, their worries, their fears,
their little heroic acts still press on and on
and your little hostel ventures and your little hostel
plays and your little commitments — all these
memories pound and grind you down

Come onto the ark my dead ones —
the one who drove us around in the carbonised nights

— David Webster
the one who committed suicide for her deserting man
— Esther Shabalala
the ones who were shot when the hostels
entered the flame years
— Phineas Zulu, Derrick Ndlovu
Come: hear my plywood creak
Tonight they say the Zulus are killing the Xhosas.

From far, where I am, where the ocean has received the
bones of those carried downstream from Nqutu
I ask my memory again —

    Chris Dlamini you were there, there were 'Zulus'
    there don't tell me it wasn't true
    Moss, you were there, when the hostels poured out
    to sign those damned forms before the offices were
    burnt in Lincoln road,
    remember? there were 'Zulus' there,
    don't tell me it wasn't true
    Peter Pheku, we walked those compounds and
    yards and you Rodney
    Mwambo, tell me, there were 'Zulus' there,
    don't tell me it wasn't true.

The past strikes at your sternum
and your plywood creaks at the joint
as your memory-ark gets
grounded tonight on the airwaves

But Death, remember, death, recollect
that your drums mr.Death
cannot scramble history's step:

I give her a little footnote, a small little footnote
that the dead of my past, that my carpenter's ark,
that my memories of hostel rooms and bunks and faces
and smoke and the grind and the strike and the cheap
loves around the back of the Vosloorus yards,
that my fading memory of hope that was, that is
still, that was, still speaks of our faces
facing the wind. I know 'Zulu' people were there,
face in the wind, the plywood creaking at the joint,
your drums mr.Death and the trumpets blasting,
I know, I hope, I hope you know I know, mr.Death.

XVI. Washing

We went down to the river
— where the dhobis used to pound
their linen with stones
where the squatter-camp people
relieved themselves before
they were removed
where our children fished —
to wash the stains from our shirts

— each stain a memory
each memory: history unstuck, chasing the ocean,
tearing down our washing-lines

we cupped our hands and drank the muddy water
as the sun scraped at our tissue
and the shirts' threading tore at our fingernails
and we scrubbed

and when they washed off
we saw our years rinse down the banks
and we cried
and when they didn't
we cried
— each stain a memory
each memory a friend.

and we closed our eyes against the glare and the light
and we prayed for the monster-wave, the monster-tidal-
wave, the largest wave, larger than all-known waves, we
prayed to some seagod to stir up this wave, to gather
the lost, the dumb, the departed worlds from the seabed
and thrust them upstream back into life;
to gather the stains, and please, remake back the loved
ones and
place them upstream

we cupped our hands and drank the muddy water
we felt other hands, cutoff,
severed hands coming downstream
and we lied they were logs
and their nails were as stiff as ours
in this monsoon time, floodtime
of our laundry days

we went down to the river
to wash the stains from our shirts
each stain a memory
each memory a friend
we felt our tired hands
departing with the others downstream
it was only our hands.

XVII. The Monkey-Tree

We are plucking out the the fires and our arms
are scabbed
the healing of wounds has been proclaimed

> So we sit dear friend under the monkey-tree again-
>> have a pawpaw
>> the war has ended
>> let's go shoeshine and piano
>> we go,

when the monkeys come
the dogs go yaowling
when the monkeys come you go
come
under the monkey-tree
again
my friend
let's talk
and then shoeshine and piano
we go

we used to laugh and throw stones
and flap about dancing, left foot up and, then the right
and listen to our visions on your box of wires
under our tree
we used to say we need a new kind of tree
to nestle our passions
like a palm with its obscene genitals at bloom
and better, a paw-paw pole added to feed our tribes
and thick tarzan ropes to swing from and bellow

and broad enough to hang a hammock
to sway our sherrywined heads
and space to leap left foot up and, then the right
and this we called our 'monkey-tree'
our mast our rudder and off we go
sugar and spice and spike
shoeshine and piano we go

and we sit here again after so many short years
so have a pawpaw
feel its bark now

and now, when the eastern storms excite the birds
and in spring
when the pollen and scent
make you scratch, or sneeze or cry
there is fear in the air
and then the monkeys return
drunk from all the perfume
and the first crescent moon
distorts all the people
    (there are horrid people near the sugar silos
    don't you go there at night
    all sugar sending places are hot
    all hot places have perfumed and rugged crowds
    and those who peg do not return to haunt you
    and if they do you can't remember them at all
    so they make futile noises just to scare you
    and then the monkeys return drunk
    and you forget them
    and you shake the tree
    and they show you their backsides
    and you tremble inside
    and you go)
come

then umngani wami, i must tell you
everynight at around sleeptime these four women come
out in dark sarries and wail
    they send shakedowns down the spines of dogs and
    humans scuttle to hide behind their comforts
they could be singing an ancient lovesong of course
but no one cares
pain is pain
scabs are scabs
they will surely be silenced, don't go.

Umngani wami, stay, it's safe here these days
I gathered your toenails and the expulsions that grow
through your scalp like hair
and mixed out of it the most potent brews
so you're safe
don't go
help me
to gather my memory that scattered
there were lovers once
we had and lost
they were hairdresser or librarian,
they had plaits
they started blonde in my dreams but turned to
orange

and I remember holding orange tufts
in my teeth and my outstretched hand
and I remember in my pocket: baboon livers and teeth.

something happened when they tore at
the sun's roots
and carved things out of its bark
and its sap was sweat or cancer.

shoeshine and piano we go
in with the burrowing termites we go
come
there's peace at last.

XVIII. Barbarism

It hurts to lose a dream — to live with the horror that
there will be no tomorrow better than our yesteryear
and our time to be marked only by this century's
register of gassed lung.

It hurts to lose a dream — we huddled in fear didn't we
up against each other, hair against hardsoft skin and
each footstep tapping the street sounded like a comma,
in that era of hope

But we took heart to dance for fierce gods — danced
on the foreground, each nerve and gesture and voice
tore at their conscience, tumbled and twisted their
moods

Took heart to dance without Him — even with
crutches we clumped at the earth with our sticknails
and heaved to ho and forward we go past the
abandoned tortoise-shells scattered on the road

Too hurt from the race to pray to him — that that god
was a good god a god that walked barefoot, a shegod, a
god that cried, that bled, that sprang off the nails

(I lost you and your promise of paradise before my first
dentures; the thereafter was postdated. I tried. I did not
give up lightly, without shudder, without pain; but I
prayed and prayed, you abandoned me early and I
prayed so hard, my eyelids so tight, tight, tight, my teeth
sunk into the opposite gums, and I worded my pleas and
my murmurs, fast, fast, fast, but you did nothing and
they marched my kin outside. I lost you in the din of the
sound that sounded like our demented neighbour
banging on his metal bath, and I murmured, please,
please, please let it be bath-bangs.

Later, I walked with cool brain past the venom people
used to die for you, cut others for you, love others for
you. I could not play abraham or hero; this creature's
breathing was the only worth we had.

I gathered furies formed by this lean and stretched hide,
perforated by visors and scanners and tinglings and tiny
liver blasts and much hair scratching for openings.

To live, then. It was written.

to write, then.

to fly, then, sail then, search then
but also to fight, then, another war
beyond despair

where a jaundiced moon turns dusk to yellow.
there: where people tear and struggle with their
dreams.)
sandlime and iron make cities and add aluminium will
conjure up cars
but I walk
there: the redmoon again
      the ochre on our shirts
      the earth that is chucked at our mouth
      to chew again
      the shacklands reach out as far as the heart can
feel

and I say once again, pointing a wearied finger, a finger
pointed by so many others so much better, perfecter
before, point it at this known world, this tired space,
this universe without dreams, this chaos of pain and say
once again, surely it is wrong to be fleeced, starved and
kicked just to feed our owner, our merchant, our
bigdadadaddy.

Susan Mabie

A Sisterhood of Resistance

A Sisterhood of Resistance

Daughters, sisters, mothers, women
when they silently persecute you
in your home, your workplace, your bedroom,
your private self:
Do not succumb.

As they drain the strength
no, not of womanhood, but of selfhood
from your gradually declining confidence:
Do not succumb.

Now that each of their silences is
an unspoken accusation
a hidden threat
a gloating mockery of your cringing self:
Do not succumb.

When succumbing seems your only hope
to give in
to vanish
to die:
Do not succumb.

Daughters, sisters, mothers, women
after yet another night of staring at the wall
and your body lies wasted and vandalised
and your eyes are aching of shed and unshed tears:
Do not succumb.

Because their victories over you
are short lived
for each assault which you refuse
to succumb to
ensures that we never will be broken.

An Old Tradition

Dusk.
The haunting Port Elizabeth wind
unsettles the old chocolate wrappings,
newspaper sheets, Checkers packets
and litter at the Korsten taxi rank.

There is no threat of rain.
There has not been one for a long time now
yet people scurry along in all directions
as if to escape the hail
of a highveld storm.

The wind peeps underneath
the skirts of huge bodies,
and unties the chastity knots
of eastern headrobes
amidst the futile attempts
to keep body and tradition in order.

You, an old man
with an old history
and an old walking stick
which helps you along an old life,
board the taxi
and nod a warm greeting to fellow travellers.

'Unjani Mama?'
in your most respectful tongue
from the days when order was the way you knew it.

Then you choke on your impassioned respect,
and cough out the cheap wine
bought at the off-sales.

You curse the loss of each drop,
as the victims of your vile disposal
curse you.

And as you try to wipe
the muck from your mouth,
you notice Mama's disapproving nod.

'Xolo Mama'
but the wind carries your message away
as the jumperboy calls Zakhele
through the open taxi window.

Sir

Sir,
my people are humble people,
we have been taught to be humble
by our ancestors.
Sir,
we do not mean to be a threat
we do not wish to harm anybody
Sir,
we ask not what does not belong to us
we try to understand others
and hope that they will understand us too.
Because sir,
my people are humble people
she said.

Sir,
my people are humble people.
but when the drums beat
blood pulses in our veins
and our ancestors talk.

They say the hand
that crushes our voices into silence
is a threat.
They say the Kasspir
that rides down our fences
is a threat.
They say that these are the forces of harm
Our ancestors say that what was theirs, is ours too.

We do not ask, what is not ours!
We do not take, what does not belong to us!
Our ancestors say that we should only understand
the message in the newborn baby's cry.

Our ancestors were humble people
Our ancestors were honest people
When the drums beat
the fire spits anger.
When the drums beat
our veins throb with angry blood.
When the drums beat
and we can no longer contain
the angry fire, the angry blood
Then we cast off all oppression
as we toyi-toyi down the road to freedom

1989 Sheila

Ghetto girl
Lost to the world that reared you
Tonight you are sprawled out
taken
Your unripe fruits of girlhood
A memory already forgotten.

In the crowded room of faces and body odours
You knew that you stood out
And your coiling body,
Thin like the reeds you once picked
Responds to the rhythms of the jive

Each movement carefully planned
skillfully performed
Seduces your brain
Surrenders your conscience.

Your breasts are hard
Each nipple razor sharp
sensitive and alert
Hard breasts respond to the pulsing beat
of your heart and stimela songs.

Ancient dances long since forgotten
by the mothers of your tribe
are remembered by you
and now carried out with seductive precision.

Your call reflects in the hungry, blank
gaze of pained male faces.

You are assured of a response
as with tight fists, throbbing heads and aching cocks
they lick their lips
and stare.

They stare at your breasts just come out
and stare at the beads of sweat
trickelling down your open shirt
disappearing where your breasts part
and they wonder what treasures
are hidden there.

As eyes penetrate your tight (very tight) white jeans
Your torso stiffens
and you lose control
over the throbbing ache between your legs.

Throbbing ache becomes longing ache
Penetrating eyes become roaming hands.

Ghetto girl
Tonight you sell your valueless chastity
Tonight you are the bride of a ghetto man.

Misty

Play misty for me tonight my love
No, not for anyone else, but play it for me.
Surround me with infinite clouds
of fleecy emptiness —
but let it be filled with beauty.
And when you play your love for me,
let the dark shades be brightened by peace;
Smoke and fire and haziness are no realities now
for we'll conform to the conventions
which you and I decide are real.
We'll forget, for a while,
about the smoking pipe
and concentrate
on escaping
into our own trip.

But the clouds are darkened
by the fires of Nyanga;
the brain deadened
by the sweet taste of poppy seeds;
And below us rages a war
kept alive by generations of certainty
that captivity can only last
as long as the voice is silent.
So should I play misty for you tonight
our tranquil love
would embrace the clouds
and release droplets of peace
to still the fire below.
So no misty tonight for you my love
For the clouds of freedom
calling from the horizon
are sweeter than the poppy joint
and shaky love.

An unfinished poem

The unfinished script burns like a crime
on my conscience
The lost idea haunts me
is a threat to my skill.

The unfinished script waits...
always waits
for an inspiration that never comes
a flash of lightning that brings with it
words, ideas
new, fresh
a masterpiece, a breakthrough
an assurance.

The unfinished script raises its ugly lines
and gloats at me
You there
the one with the pen in her hand;
Yes you
the one with the pen
with all the ink
which can not write
Yes you
Finish this script,
if you can!

The unfinished script, my unfinished guts
patiently mocks my dumb stare
painfully questions my verbal bloc
The unfinished script waits...
waits for an assurance
which I do not have.

Untitled

You and I
are not special
we are particles of countless
grains of sand
tramped upon
walked over
by people like us
and one of the millions
of droplets of water
forever floating
as the tide beckons
Your face is but a brick in the wall
of the white collar corps
I am but one of the dresses
wolf whistled at
we, mass production replicas
For you and I are not special
despite the life
created by us alone
still we are not special
Because in shacks and mansions
in townships and suburbs

there are others
like us
who have created new lives
and now revel
like we do
in this knowledge of miracles
and are now troubled
like we are
to anxious days of wonder
about the beauty or doom of it all
So you and I are not special
we are one of the floating masses
and faceless
not special.

Untitled

No! it was not
when on the Freudian Couch
you drew your guts and shot it
against the wall
(like a Shane of the nineties)
for shrinks to see
and telescopically analyse
that you were honest.

Yet you believed in yourself
for what else could you do?

It was in your moments of silence
and your voice pitched too high

with your eyes refusing to make contact
that your honesty showed
and although you did not know it
you spoke the message of love
and hate
with the clarity of your desired crystal glass.

Siphiwe Ka Ngwenya

To Celebrate is a Must

To Celebrate is a Must

We have gathered here to celebrate
To celebrate the cracking whip that keeps the ball rolling
To celebrate the ravaging of women's virginity
To celebrate the falling spear of manhood
To celebrate raging death supping with our beloved ones
For to celebrate is a must

I want to hang my poems on a washing line
To make them dry out like ostrich biltong
Or like a defeated boxer hanging up his gloves
Engulfed by eyes taken aback
Not because the opponent is tough
But the spirits said: enough is enough

I want to rip my poems to bleed blood
Like a wild dog ripping a cat into countless pieces
To let the world inhale an odourous smell
This world a dog's carcass a slum's bucket-system
This world sniffing teargas as if it's snuff
This trigger-happy world dancing to machine-gunning

Celebrate oldness before the cock crows
Celebrate this time of niknaks
That pensions poets from poetry
Backing away slowly to early days like tortoises
Dancing, caressing and yelping as people gallop with pain
The so-called fence sitters

Let my poetry sit on the fence
Even if they say a fence is electrified or barbed wired

I am tired of penning words of pain
For people who stand motionless when our tears roll
For people who are blind to see blood flooding
For people who are not touched when someone is raped
For people who laugh when death knocks at their doors

Tell me not about poetry
Poetry fiddling with images
A poet gagging people as i do
A poet police-forcing people to be pierced as i am
Give me heart transplants for those who are heartless
Give me brain transplants for those who are brainless

Let me propose love to the art of war
Like a black bard
Coughed out from the chimney smoke of phiri
That squeezes me like a rotten potato
Away from my haunted brothers
Who could stick a knife into someone's heart
Just for a cent
To make me pack my suitcase & go

I am packing my suitcase now
In the match-box of dlamini
Which hides flashbacks
Where my umbilical cord is buried
Prancing to school with my black and white uniform
Dancing away the dust from my black shoes
To be fed with education which benzines our minds
Never did my father tell me
Never did my silent mother tell me
That education for me is a key to prison
Maybe suspecting that the boil would burst

I am dipping my feet into this fuggy road
I am pattering the pricking sand
To throw the rocks of moshoeshoe
To make this world the world of davids and golliaths
To play soccer on a mini-ground
Not the ball which makes screamer shiver
Succumbing to evils of the night
The night which spanks thighs of young girls
The night which baby-kiss young boys
While whispering transparent promises

Where is bra zinga
Remember memory is a weapon
The memory of kofifi
The memory of district six
The memory of kwa-bhanya
Memory is a spear that never stops spearing
Memory is a gun that never stops dumdumming
Go on
Rise moshoeshoe cetshwayo sekhukhuni makana rise all
My chest is now flexing
My wrinkled face is now frowning
My voice whistles like the movement of indlondlo
Rise-up

Rise-up
It's time for the black power salute
Time to dance to azikhwelwa blues
Which made vorster shout white power
When hector peterson's clenched fist said black power
Time to prance to the murderous bullets
That summoned soweto children to death

When frowning at gutter education
To our future dark and desolate
To make the azure sky blaze with fire
I was only a toddler

I am packing it   pack & move
As a todder I knew encumberment
Oh mama come back to me
Let your spirit abide with me
Oh mama let death not take you away from me
When i carry boxes at j.maddison & sons
While baas tuis bellowed racist insults
I want to glue my father's mouth
Who thought umlungu mkhulu
Making my clenched fist shrink like a lollipop
Do you still want me to take off my hat
Do you still want me to kneel down
I will not wait for another clap

I will march to the mountains of humanity
To dream in the land of bleeding ancestors
Oh arise mathong'amahle
I want thoko to cleanse my heart
She who climbed the mountain of my heart
But susan opened her nubile heart
Her womb feeling the burden of poppy & nonkululeko
Her nubile heart which blinkered my mind
Oh lelizwe linomoya

I stumbled
To temco
Succumbing to soldier games

Shrugging my shoulders to bossy games
Where people laugh with their teeth
Where people hide their hearts in garbage-bins
Where tribalism knocks
Where retrenchments bang
Like at impala stationery
When i went back home in the dark
To embrace my beloved ones with sweat
The embrace diminishing the anger of toiling
Tell me
How many times do i have to tell you
Are you deaf and dumb

Are you deaf and dumb
That you can't recall those soldiers buzzing like flies
Heavily armed to a funeral of a six-year old boy
Cause his spirit still lives
Those soldiers who made us duck dance and dive
To teargas and rubber-bullets
Those soldiers who returned to the bereaved's house
To back-pay us with fear
Fear of drowning in that quicksand like this boy

Cats are meauing
And i want to run
Yes baba peter setuke   i shall run if you tell me to
To run like a marathon runner
To run further than a marathon runner
Like that coke which made me collide with bullets
Dum-dum-dum i thought it was a drum
The drum which made the coke bottle crush on the gravel
As i told my feet to abba me to safety

I leaped fences like a cat
And dogs ceased barking
To them i was just a bucket-system terrorist
To be disarmed of my humanity
By mouths vomiting humility

Look at them   look
Dogs are shying away
As if caught eating eggs
Like those black sweating faces
At moroka police station
Anger scribbled on their faces
But they are nothing crushed long ago
My mind still burns   it burns
From those flames of humiliation
And my heart still bleeds   it bleeds
From those scars of innocence
Kill me now

Kill me now
As i walk home
As i walk along the pavement
Kill me now
As i walk through the streets
Kill me now
For i cannot fly away like a bird
Even birds fly and come down
I want to walk at home
Before this home walks on me
I want to walk on this pavement
Before this pavement walks on me
I want to walk in these streets

Before these streets walk on me
On this road
This road
A long road
A passage road
A narrow road
A knifing road
A wailing road

Kill me now
Kill me quick   i charge you
Move me now
Move me quick   i charge you
My nose is sniffing blood
My eyes are as fiery as death
My chest is blazing like the sky

I will not die with folded arms
It is said agostino neto used a pen and the machine
But me i have no machine
I have only a voice and a pen
I shall make my voice the machine
There is no use yearning for the spear
When it ends with your breath coming from your lips
Your anger is melting like ice
Your anger is bookish
You don't care about
Those speared and assegaid at nhlazane and merafe
Those who kissed the dust in sebokeng
Those perpetuating broedertwis in bekkersdal
Kill me now,
No the spear has not yet fallen

I am the spear
I shall grieve and
I shall grieve no more

I shall grieve no more
To handprints stained with blood
Blood of our children maimed
Blood of your husbands tamed
Blood of your wombs chained
Cry no more
Cry not like babies wailing for milk
Drink your tears and blood
Tears wrinkling your face
Blood reddening your pace till your limbs of struggle are cut
Till your limbs of struggle dumdums like bullets
Bullets that riddle your burden
The burden that dreams the light
Of peace of unity of justice
Give me a voice, a pen, paper
To echo my feelings
When the road to freedom is bleak
Give it a break
To make me celebrate
Without shedding any tears
Zanele i assure you

Celebrate   shed no tears
Even if vipers bite
Let your teargassed eyes have sight
As you hasten to be sardined in third-class trains
Or bundled in windowless buses
Families knowing only goodbye and goodnight kisses

Your lives hammered by those whose appetites
Are whetted by hatred
I hear your voices shouting   ndzirilo manano
Listen to its echo

Listen to its echo
The whip is cracking
Bundling us to slavery in cattle-trucks
Dumped like pigs in tin-shacks
Blacklisted bards bullied on benches
Digesting words rhyming with lashes
Shanties fiercely demolished
By minds so demonic
That angry women stripped in dobsonville

Celebrate   shed no tears
It is only a willow that weeps
Just take a trip to prison without fears
Where walls of anguish converse as if they have lips
Where chains chant rhythmically
Making you raise your atrophied muscles
And gnaw the bone of oppression
Which smells of gunpowder
Now that i am here

I am here with you
Duduzile will you please heal my wounds
Make my life rosier than roses
With your face as bright as daylight
With your eyes that twinkle brighter than stars
Move african giraffe

To foresee africa reborn
In this men-only compartments where i slumber
Men talk like buzzing flies
Denying me a song, your song
You song bird who made me feel a bang
In the hiroshima of my heart
And the nagasaki of my mind
With fierce darts piercing

Are my feelings natural
I heard ma-kwadi saying there is nothing natural
Let me not post my affections in the dark
Affections that blur our vision
Delving deep into us with confusion
I feel the hands of your heart embalming
And summer advancing
Go on   climb this freedom wagon

Climb this freedom wagon
Africa think
Just up your guts, guts-up
Guts-up
For those tripped to death in botswana
For those swallowed by bullets in swaziland
For those who danced to their graves in lesotho
For the 'let them come' of zambia
For those who preferred railway-lines
I know about sharpeville   soweto   langa
I know about kathlehong   duduza   mamelodi
I know about those who shunned their houses in thokoza
I know about the middle-east-like war of natal
The fight has been declared
A technical draw

Our bloodied fight was just a stray-bullet
Which made aghett kiss the struggle goodbye
Which blessed hector peterson with death
Which robbed braam fischer of life
Which struck david webster down
The david and golliath brawl has been declared invalid
Go south african like a selling product

Go south african like a selling product
I am also climbing out of the morass
My eyes shrink slowly   slowly
I pity you, yoliswa
Just hold my hand and let me take you out with this poem
My eyes won't strip you naked
Do you fear they can read your mind
Do you fear they can read your heart
Are you still frightened by these
Eyelashes closing like curtains
My debased face becoming cloudy
With the nerves of my body jangled
By the hidden eye of the summer sun
Which floats my mind into a sea of slumber
My heart crawls like a toddler
My skiny body melts into jelly

My feet perspire
And my dry lips expire
With my throat thirsty for water
My arms folded on the table
And i fell asleep
It is raining oh

Oh it is raining
I wish my body was waterproof
As we trudge the road
From marabastad to winterveld
Ben drenched
Me drenched
Thunder or lightning we had to trudge the road
Shed no tears

Shed no tears
For the damn curfew
Everywhere everyone is talking about this curfew
Stop   stop raping our dreams
Why rape and say
Africa was enticing you   seducing you
As you said when raping africa
Africa was dark and we brought spotlights
To make savages stop eating fruits of eden
And to make their lives urban
Never bubble about urbanity
When exiles yell for indemnity
Now
While we are asleep with the snoring sun
You who parade our streets with the moon
To hell with you
Lest we collide in the night
Go this way i shall go that way
I am beginning to barricade the doors of my heart
So not to be caught in your fruitless inertia
Where the tuinhuis becomes a puinhuis
Bubbling about a new south africa
Forgetting when the old was miscarriaged

To cage us in this mythical den
Where our freedom is whipped
Forcing us to nourish the boorish five-year plan
Even my kitchen cochroaches have a sad tale to tell

To troop ecstasies of joy
Planted by an effusion
Leading us into an illusion
My people want to dance
Dance dance dance to groove me baby
They want to get down
To drink
To eat
To sleep
They want to forgive and forget
In bed with disco & shebeen women
Who aren't afraid to jump from bed to bad
With men who aren't afraid to whore
Just to prove they are masculine
For the ghetto to labour children we abhor
Children born fatherless & motherless
With only pavemenets and parks to sleep
Just stay indoors   you are all sheep
For the sake of population explosion
Hold me african woman

Hold me
Stand firm and make me see beauty
I want to listen without feeling guilty
I hear a trumpet blaring
As i peep at your killing laugh
While lowering your edblo-hand to be kissed

Easing my heart's flames
With my sore lips feeling the magnet
As your voice utters a tearing goodbye
Leaving me with a sigh
Something electrocuting my hands
While caressing your palms
I am raising my blinking eyes
To watch your raven hair waving
And feel the ointment of freedom embalming
Your berry-face
your twinkling eyes thorned my brain
I want to hold your hand covered in dashiki
To listen to a drumming tabor on your thighs
As my eyes leapfrog to your lip-iced lips
Which shamed my sore and dry lips
What magnet do you have to tickle my heart   tell me
Making my eyes follow you like a shadow
As you pranced like a peacock to the door
With the thirsty eyes of men freezing on the floor
Their libido minds in stony calm
Waiting to be palmolived in your barbed wired heart
Please hold me tight

Hold me tight please
I am dying
I am falling from a tenth-storey building
Hold me tight
I am hanging myself with a shoelace
Please hold me tight
I am dying
I am slipping on a piece of soap
Hold me tight

I am killing myself with books
Please hold me tight
I am dying
I am killing myself with poetry
Please sing me a song
Someone is pointing a bloodied finger at me
Oh   i am running now
I hear their dogs barking
Their torches blinding my eyes
Oh i am running now
They are coming now
Hold me please
I have reached a cul-de-sac
How can i stop thinking about you

How can i stop thinking about you
I long to see you
Mpho and nkosinathi brothers and friends
I see you in your loneliness
Receiving voortrekkershoogte prison curls
Not soothing your brotherly wounds
Engulfed by clanking chains
Encumbering you with the fatigue of toiling
Your families drumming a sad rhythm
Look at our streets now in melancholy
What about the jokes we cracked in mohiyeni street
And the courting of beauties
And amagenge flying with cars in the dust
As you now holiday in prison
Outside you would have been donors of blood
To these vampires bleeding this earth
Unmask yourselves for inkululeko is born
Give me a pen and a paper

Give me a pen and paper
They have ringed the siren
In this new south african groove oh groove me baby
But others want a boerestaat just like the vrystaat
Let the new south africa suckle the ink of my pen
Like a baby suckling milk from a mother
Mother of africa
Mother of the world
Get down

Get deep down
And pick up the tree's tap-roots
I am not trying to rhyme
To hammer critics who kill your spirit
Who dub your creativity rhetoric
It's poetic in our hissing streets

Tell me
Is this country apartheid-enough to be of poetic taste
Well that is only for intellectual waste
But remember sonqoba
We shall besiege the garrisoned doors of liberation
For in our afforested streets our feelings are oral
And voiced as moral

Research in the island of your intellect
For you resemble
These blood-thirsty hippoes roaming township streets
Streets that have watching leaves
Leaves that do not platter
To the iron fist that flatter
Get down

559 ❖ Siphiwe Ka Ngwenya

I wish my granny was here
Mamama please come to us
Don't waste your tears for the blood of craig duli
Come and narrate those ancient stories of sharks
That could spit at you in the parks

I only want to be a citizen
To be a citizen is to be a hobo
In serote's city johannesburg
Than being called a poet
A hobo who can't even change the world
Who only worry about food and sleep
To pester tourist
And sleep in pipes
And make love on pavements and in parks

I want to be an inhuman registered hobo
To peel apartheid propaganda like a banana
To shame bright lights of the city
Whipping us in the black & white streets without pity
Yes a hobo
And wear dingy clothes
And wear tattered clothes
And bath myself with dung
And patter oppression with barefeet
And perfume so-called civilization with odour
And plague the people
Tell me
What are you going to do
About me
A hobo

Even when i go to rainbow five
There is no rainbow
Maybe it is waiting for me at avalon cemetery
Because nowadays our lives are as cheap as death
Cause we toss them like dice
Love is like falling from a step-ladder i tell you
Reminds me of days gone by
When freedom drums echoed
like mamokhele's heart beat
When love came like lightning
Go on blow the soil

Go on blow the soil
Get down blow it
Never forget to kiss the soil
Like sam nujoma
Like andimba toivo ja toivo
Me, i want to blow the soil with my poetry
With my whinning words
Making the repressive army to fall like flies
For decades they have been humming lies

Let the people flex their hearts
Let them be prisoners of hope
Let them raise their clenched fists
And stamp their pattering feet
Go on
Let the african sun talk

Let the african sun talk
Talk like a talking drum
Oh beat

Marimba
Mbira
Conga
And let the people dance
It's time to celebrate

Dance dance dance
To sculptures of makonde
And prance
To the ronga(tsonga) and zwide's incwala ceremony
Remove
Remove these bundles of sticks
Around bottle-curved waistes of balete women
Go on, go

Go on
Blow the soil get down
Never forget to seal it
For the fiery liberation should remain lit
I want to taste paints of thami ka mnyele
Whose body was riddled with dumdum bullets
By the trigger-happy finger that mows
I want to listen to songs of vuyisile ka mini
As he marched to the gallows

Let me celebrate
I want to eat umbhaqanga
I want to dance to umbhaqanga
Before i march to open graves in the name of indlamu
Indlamu & traditional weapons killing people
in the name of peace
In this epoch of screeching hippoes

In this pizza civilization
Where poets sweat for poetic license
In this a tearing renaissance
And make the system mad
Leaving the iron fist sad
To make the country a tin
And the people sardines
Can commercials seduce us
Like a woman advertising mum deodorant
But now it seems to be spraying us
Like someone spraying pests with baygone green
To keep the country clean
And use stayfree as a slogan
Go on, go

Go on
Blow the soil, blow it
For soweto, without norweto
Norweto killed when still in an unknown womb
For soweto i shall sing
Soweto where i rest
Soweto where i jest
In your dusty streets i shall dance
To taste teargas
To kiss venomous bullets
Do you remember soweto by night
Soweto my final weapon
A weapon that could massacre crocodile tears
A weapon that could smite the smile
Soweto garden of eden
Eden not on the map of freedom
Soweto decorated with strange trees
That blossom with police-stations and troop-trucks

Soweto at times you terrify me
Soweto at times you horrify me
Like the matebeleland battle fields
Or the west bank with its grave of toddlers
Making them children of death
What are in these i love soweto stickers

Rise-up mothers
Rise-up like the intifada
Rise-up and give birth to culture
Instill knowledge in the people
Soweto my future our future
I won't ask who i am

I won't ask who i am
For who i am i am
I am child of africa
Painfully laboured in the veld of the world
To be chained in this ugly world
Like jesu
Whom it is claimed was crucified
For sweet nothing
I am africa
I am nkululeko
I am amandla

Let me remove your heart cause you are heartless
Let me remove your face cause you are faceless
You have no feelings
You have thrown african roots to the sea
You have cursed your ancestors
You are transparent like a mini-skirt

Let me remove dung from your ears
Let me remove sawdust from your eyes
And unlock your brain
Before the call
The call that makes a finger click a trigger
A trigger that releases a bullet
A bullet that dumdums our hearts
Hearts toyi-toying with a coffin shoulder-high
Shoulder-high to the cemetery
As children we never tasted joy
Our lives have been kicked like a ball
Let the mountain fall
Let us have a joll
Let's dance

Let's dance to the trombone of jonas gwangwa
To be soaked in marabi blues
Now as i hear masekela's trumpet blaring
Making me shriek to fergusson's piano
Beat the drum
The drum of thobejane
Sing, tshidi leloka, sing
Sing, portia qubeka, sing
Sing, thembi mtshali, sing
Sing, sophie mgcina, sing
I want to hear your sweet voices breezing
I want to stand like a statue on our black stoep
And watch people passing by like tired cattle
And watch goddesses passing by
And laugh at amagenge prancing in the streets
Saying viva to beer & sminorff
And watch lovers ignoring rain raining
The rain that could strengthen their love

Everything seems as bright as daylight
I see young and old burdening
themselves with buckets full of water
I heard men buzzing and women yelping
But that was not a baptism of fire

I want you to sing a song without any fear
Sing sing my people lizobuya sing
Sing sing my people zabalaza sing
Sing a song worth singing
Sing the welela song of miriam makeba
The welela song still flooded with soweto blues
Mam'umakeba please hold me tight
Let us together go and fetch izinkomo
Haven't you heard sakhile shouting phambili

I want you to sing a song with cheers
Sing sing maqabane sing
Sing sing madelakufa sing
Africa you who no more bow down
to the clap-clap of oppression
Removed the barbed wires from our brains
Africa, sukuma thayima

And let us dance
To the beat of the drum
From the drum this drum
The drum of the gods

This is the drum of the gods
The drum is throbbin
The drum is born

The drum of the people
The drum of onoura mutabaruka lkj
The drum of barney wailer, yellowman, i-roy
The drum of cortez, joseph, jara

The drum is drummin
The drum is on
The drum of celebration
The drum of sakhile, amampondo, wasamata, kerkorrel
The drum of bayete, sankomota, coyote
The drum of letta mbuli, semenya, pongola
The drum of jambo, positive vibes
The drum of fela, kaita chinx

The drum is beatin
The drum is not gone
The drum for a new south africa
The drum blowin like the wind
Wavin like leaves
Shakin like the stem
Flexin like branches
Bleedin like roots
The drum wailin like the earth

Now that oil in the gulf is to ooze like blood
The oil that drowns iraq in kuwait
While israeli bullets mow down palestinians
In jerusalem's temple mount
Worshippers are thrown with rocks

Like water boiling from the kettle of kenya
Burning buttocks of nairobi
Like british rockets rocking lybia
Like british gongs gagging argentina
Like the stinging bullet shreading martin luther's dream

This is a new world they say
First world
Second world
Third world
New world
New world to witness star wars
To witness the dancing skeletons in the horn of africa
Where people yearn for an utopia
But shunning ethiopia
Ethiopia scattered like the mutilated body of doe
Sing sbongile khumalo sing
Sing sekunjalo sing
Sing never cry tears

Never cry tears
To wrinkle your swollen faces
Sinking knees of the old are standing
Standing knees of the old are bending
To be robbed of their pension
From a snake-queue which makes them yell
To the cracking whip of the sun
To be pensioned with pain
Sing
Sing them a pension song that is as long as a snake
Dance, prance, write

Dance
Prance
Write
Write the writing on the wall
For graffitti days are numbered
Numbered on this
black
green and
gold
graffitti

I shall sing
Till my voice goes hoarse
I shall sing a song with my vibrating lips
This song is for the world

I shall sing
To kiss away my own tears
I shall kiss away my own tears

I heard that a new world has beamed like the shy sun
From the wailing perestroyka
To the howling pretoriastroika
To our land as young as an old bird
I am stretching my hands
Like the sun rising from the sea
I want to fly back home
I am homeward bound now
Like a nomadic bird
I shall fly back home
Over dark and desolate valleys
Dark valley

Desolate valley
Where cats sleep next to bonfires
Where children's faces are maps of drying tears
Their dingy bodies resembling their tattered clothes
But it's time to go home
To the arms of my mother
To the arms of my father
Are you there my brothers and sisters
To welcome me to this frowning land
The land which makes my body like a voice in trimolo
Home i shall go

Home i shall go
Now or never
To be stabbed by the dirty sore lips of children
To dance with the hurricane dust
Like my father dancing and shuffling on the floor
In front of my jubilant mother
After drinking a calabash of umqombothi
& a glass of lion lager
I shall listen to the chirping of crickets
The hooting of owls
Trumpeting the gospel of struggle
Blowing the horn of liberation
My horn, your horn, our horn

Let us all stand firm
Firm like umyezane tree
Awaiting for all caged birds to be set free
Free like exiled birds to be welcomed back home
I have touched the hands of a few
Even those exiled within the land of their birth
Free not like tsevetanka's image of an opened prison

Home
I am standing at home
Waiting and waiting
Waiting for the fallen to rise up from their shaking graves
To sing
Sing
To dance
Dance
Without any tears
Tears no
Tears shall freeze like ice-cubes
Let us sing away our hatred
Sing till our voices get hoarse

Dance like the feet of thembi nyandeni
Dance like the feet of nomsa manaka
Dance like the feet of nobantu
Dance like the feet of sizakele
Dance like the feet of fikile
Dance like the feet of sipho mchunu
Dance like the feet of jonny clegg
Dance like the feet of james chitukuta
Dance like the feet of selloane
Dance you gumboot dancers
Dance till your knees go jelly
Halala... fela kutiiii....
This is customs check point
Celebrate
Till death intervenes
From these words
My words, your words, our words
Strutting on this road
To open this gate of a new decade

Biographical Notes on the Contributors

PETER ANDERSON was born in Johannesburg in 1949. His father, a weight-lifter and wrestler who wrote a sentimental novel called *Minnie Minnaar*, had secret ambitions to sing like Caruso, but made a living as a telephone linesman; his mother, who had dreamt of being a schoolteacher, was a worker in a garment factory in Doornfontein.

In Anderson's view, the explicit politics required of poets under apartheid has been a 'facilitative obstacle: the glass ceiling to what we can say, but at the same time an incitement to put a fist through the glass'. On a Fulbright Scholarship to America since 1988, he is at present doing a Ph.D. in English at Boston University.

LISA COMBRINCK was born in Cape Town in 1967. She was educated at Harold Cressy High School and at the University of Cape Town where she received a BA (HONS) degree in African Studies. She is currently completing an MA on South African short stories at the University of Cape Town. She has written stories since childhood, but only began writing poetry from the age of sixteen.

Her work has been published in magazines and anthologies. She has read and performed her work at cultural forums in the Cape. She has organized and participated in cultural activities over the past ten years in cultural, civic and youth structures, and in recent years has been involved in editing and education in the Western Cape region of COSAW.

MARK ESPIN was born in Cape Town in 1964. He matriculated from Cathkin High School and studied at the University of the Western Cape during 1984 and 1985. At present he is employed as a clerk in Bellville and lives in Athlone. His poems have previously been published in *Contrast, Ekapa, Upstream, New Coin, Staffrider, Horses: Athlone* and *I Qabane Labantu*.

PATRICK FITZGERALD was born in 1954. He went to school in Germiston and Johannesburg and later attended the University of the Witwatersrand. While at Wits he was involved in cultural affairs, co-founding both the Box Theatre and the Junction Avenue Theatre Company. Active in student politics, he was vice-President of the Students Representative Council in 1976 and a well-known 'library lawns' orator. In 1977 he was General-Secretary of the National Union of South African Students (NUSAS) and underwent detention without trial during this period.

He lived in exile in Gaborone, Botswana from 1979 to 1984 where he was active in the MEDU Art Ensemble, working on the editorial board of the *MEDU Newsletter*. From 1985 until 1989 he worked as Administrative Secretary of the African National Congress Department of Arts and Culture in Lusaka, Zambia (doing some studying in the UK in between). During this period he read his poetry in a variety of countries including Angola, Tanzania, the Soviet Union, Brazil, Holland, Tanzania and Norway.

He is presently a senior lecturer at Wits University and Co-ordinator of the new Public & Development Management Programme in the Faculty of Management.

KEITH GOTTSCHALK was born 1946 and lives in Cape Town. He works in the Political Studies Department at the University of the Western Cape and is a founder member of COSAW who served on its Western Cape and national executives.

Ninety-two of his poems have been published over three decades in magazines and anthologies. A few have been published in Uganda, the UK, USA and Germany, and some translated into Xhosa, Italian, German and French. Keith hopes to someday publish his own collection. He writes: 'The dynamics of over seventy performances to usually working-class Cape audiences encouraged some of my poems to be more multi-lingual in Xhosa and Afrikaans — even if my cross-over and non-conformist styles make some literary establishments choke!'

He is currently experimenting with a cycle of space flight poems.

SIPHIWE KA NGWENYA was born in 1964 at Phiri (Soweto). He attended school at Senaoane Secondary School where he matriculated in 1983. He was a teacher for a short spell at Ndondo H.P. School and worked as General Assistant at Transvaal Envelope Manufacturing Company (TEMCO). He was a student of African Literature and History at Khanya College in 1987. He is a member of the African Writers Association and presently a member of the Congress of South African Writers and the Performing Arts Workers Equity. He studied drama at the Federated Union of Black Artists. He has participated in literary and performance activities locally and abroad, won but never received a prize for a poem 'I Have a Dream', organised by the King-Luthuli Transformation Centre sponsored by the Martin Luther Foundation. He works part-time as a translator and is working on another epic poem titled 'Melody of Our Last Harvest'.

BALEKA KGOSITSILE was born in Durban on 24 September 1949. She started to compose songs and poems when she was ten years and crossed the Tyumie River regularly from Fort Hare — where her father was a librarian — to Lovedale where she went to school.

Her poetry was published while she was in exile in *Malibongwe, Rixaka, Somehow we Survive, AACC Bulletin* and other publications. Her first manuscript of poetry *I Want to be an Echo* is yet unpublished. She has written some short stories, one of which 'In the Night' was published in a collection of stories by African women brought out by SIDA to coincide with the end of the UN Decade for Women, 1985.

From 1983 she was a member of the Writers and Music Units of MEDU Art Ensemble and was its head when the SADF raid on Gaborone disrupted its work. She was a member of the Southern African Arts Trust Fund and currently serves on the COSAW Editorial Collective.

She is Secretary General of the African National Congress Women's League and sits on the ANC Negotiations Commission and National Executive Committee. She is a mother of five children and is married to Keorapetse Kgositsile.

DEELA KHAN was born in Elsies River, Cape Town, on 25 February 1954. After completing her primary education in

1966, she left school in 1967 and worked as a shop assistant for the following decade. In 1977 she began to attend Adult Education classes and matriculated in 1981 after which she worked as a travel clerk.

She started studying English and Psychology through Unisa, in 1984 and completed her degree majoring in English and History at the University of the Western Cape in 1988. She obtained her BA Honours in English in 1991. She writes poetry and short stories.

ALLAN KOLSKI HORWITZ was born in 1952 in Vryburg. He grew up in Cape Town and studied philosophy and literature at the University of Cape Town. In 1974, he left South Africa living in Israel, Britain and the United States, before returning in 1986 to live in Johannesburg where he joined the Hotel and Restaurant Workers Union as an organizer. He is currently a national co-ordinator in SACCAWU (South African Commercial Catering and Allied Workers Union). He has published a collection of poetry entitled *Call from the Free State* (1979) and has been published in *Staffrider* and *New Coin*.

RUSTUM KOZAIN was born in Paarl in 1966 and grew up there as well. He enrolled at the University of Cape Town in 1985 and has been at this institution ever since. At present he tutors in the Department of English and is reading towards an MA degree. His thesis is entitled 'Contemporary English Oral Poetry by Black Poets with Particular Reference to Great Britain and South Africa'.

His main academic interests are politics, popular culture, contemporary music and literature and how these inter-connect. He is also editor of *Imago*, a student poetry publication, and winner of the Nelson Mandela Poetry Prize for 1989 at UCT. He has had poetry published in *Imago*, *Staffrider*, *Akal*, and *Under Lansdown Bridge*.

MATTHEW KROUSE was born in Germiston in 1961 and later studied Theatre at the University of the Witwatersrand.

He was a founder member of Weekend Theatre, Possession Arts, City Theatre and Dance Company and Re-Action Group.

He co-authored and performed in the following plays: *Famous Dead Man* (1986); *Active Pleasure* (1987); *Sunrise City* (1988); *Score Me the Ages* (1989).

He co-authored and designed the Weekend Theatre film *Shot Down* (1986); as well as two short films *Die Voortrekkers* (1987) and *The Soldier* (1989).

Most of this work in theatre and film has been, and remains, banned by the State censors.

His writing has appeared in *Staffrider*, *New Coin Poetry*, *Porno Literature*, *Spark*, and *Vrye Weekblad*.

Presently, he works for COSAW Publishers and is editing a forthcoming anthology of Lesbian and Gay writing.

SUSAN MABIE was born in Kimberley. She was educated at the University of the Western Cape and holds a BA (HONS) degree in English. She was an English school teacher for two years and presently works as the Eastern Cape Regional Co-ordinator of the Congress of South African Writers.

Mabie, an outspoken exponent of feminist movement issues in South African literature, is currently working with a collective compiling an anthology of *Contemporary Women's Writing* to be published by COSAW shortly.

MZIKAYISE MAHOLA was born in Claremont, Durban in 1949 and grew up with his grandmother in Lushington near Alice in the Eastern Cape. In 1962 he rejoined his parents in Port Elizabeth. He completed his high school education at Lovedale and Healdtown Colleges. His education at Fort Hare University was disrupted by financial and political factors.

He joined the Port Elizabeth-based Isihlobo Youth Group where he began writing poetry. His early work was confiscated by the Security Police which led to what he refers to as a 'spiritual death' in him and his group. In 1988 he started writing again.

His work has since been published in a number of journals. He currently lives in Port Elizabeth where he works as an assistant marine biologist for the Port Elizabeth Museum.

FRANK MEINTJIES was born in Pietermaritzburg. He studied at the Universities of the Western Cape and Natal. Between 1981 and 1984 he worked as a journalist for the *Natal Witness*. From 1986 to 1989 he was Information Officer of the Congress of South African Trade Unions.

He started writing at school and has published poetry in *Staffrider* and essays, reviews and columns in *New Nation*, *Weekly Mail* and *South*. His short stories have appeared in *Tribute* and *Ingolovane*. In 1990 he co-edited a special edition of *Staffrider* on *Worker Culture*. He presently works for the Community-Based Development Project at the University of the Witwatersrand.

LANCE NAWA, alias Earl Bean, was born in Lady Selbourne, and later moved to Hammanskraal after the former racially-integrated neighbourhood of Pretoria was demolished. He received a BA (HONS) in Sociology from the University of Cape Town and also recently 'dropped-out' from a masters programme at Northwestern University, Illinois, USA.

Earl Bean is the author of *Muso-poetry Perched on Live Wires*. A pragmatist, existentialist, his other works have appeared in several publications, including *Voices from Young Africa*, *Icarus*, *Staffrider*, *Ingolovane*, *Ja-nee*, *Upbeat*, *New Nation*, *Tribute*, and *Spring is Rebellious*. Now a book-reviewer for *New Nation* and a contributing editor for *Staffrider*, Nawa also wrote for *Weekly Mail*, *South* and *Bona* magazine.

Bean-boy is a nomad but can be found, most of the times, in Eersterust, Pretoria.

MXOLISI M. NYEZWA was born in 1967 in New Brighton, Port Elizabeth. He is a founder-member of the Imvaba Cultural Society. In 1985 he wrote an unpublished play, *Mother and Child*.

He has published poetry in literary journals, both local and abroad like the *New Coin*, *Upstream*, *Staffrider*, *New Contrast* and in popular newspapers like the *New Nation*, *Grocott's Mail* and in magazines like *Tribute*.

BARBARA SCHREINER grew up and went to school and university in Pietermaritzburg. She has lived in Johannesburg since 1981 except for some years spent in England where she did an MA in creative writing. She has published *My Spirit is not Banned*, the story of Frances Baard, as well as several poems and short stories. She has co-authored three plays, the most recent of which, 'Endangered Species', was performed at the Edinburgh Festival, the Zabalaza Festival and the Sechaba Festival in Glasgow, in 1990. She is an active member of COSAW and the ANC.

MORAKABE SEAKHOA was born at the end of the Fifties in the small village of Uitkyk in Lichtenburg in the South-western Transvaal.

He grew up and schooled in Evaton and Sebokeng townships in the Vaal Triangle. After completion of his schooling he was imprisoned for five years on Robben Island and released in 1984. He was subsequently detained for several long spells, spending much of his time in solitary confinement.

He started writing in the mid-1970s. He has published some of his poems in magazines, an anthology called *Scenes from Another Day*, one short story in *Mayibuye* and *Spark* journals. He also has two of his poems set to music by Vusi Mahlasela for his recently released debut album *When You Come Back Home*.

After his release from Robben Island, he became an organiser for the Vaal Civic Association. He has also worked as a reporter for the then *SASPU National* (now *Spark*) magazine, as the Vaal organiser for the now defunct United Democratic Front (UDF), as education officer for the then Commercial Catering and Allied Workers Union of South Africa (CCAWUSA) and the then SAYCO-affiliated STYCO (Southern Transvaal Youth Congress) as education co-ordinator.

He has been Transvaal Regional Co-ordinator for the Congress of South African Writers since 1989.

RUSHDY SIERS was born in 1952 in District Six. His family, and the rest of the community were forcefully removed in the late 1960s. He has been actively involved in cultural, civic and labour politics from his school days. He presently works at the Centre for Development Studies at the

University of the Western Cape.

He has published the *No-Act Play: A Cycle of Poetry*, short stories and poetry in numerous anthologies. He is a fellow of the University of Iowa International Writers School.

ARI SITAS was born in 1952. He is the Co-ordinator of the Centre for Industrial & Labour Studies at the University of Natal. Apart from industrial studies, Sitas has been involved in creative work since the mid-1970s. He cut his teeth in the theatre as a co-founder of the Junction Avenue Theatre Company where he was involved in many of its productions.

He has been very active in the development of worker theatre on the Reef and in Natal. Apart from writing, directing, facilitating and sometimes acting in the theatre, he has been writing poems and prose. His first collection of poetry *Tropical Scars* was published by COSAW in 1989. This was followed by *William Zuyu — A Xmas Story*, a novella published in 1991 by Buchu Books.

MAVIS SMALLBERG was born in Cape Town some while ago, grew up and lived on the Cape Flats practically all her life. She trained as a teacher and taught Physical Education to very enthusiastic pupils at a local primary school before leaving for London where she did a course in Creative Dance at the Laban Art of Movement Studio. Since then she has taught Dance and Physical Education at a school in Manenberg and a teacher training institution in Cape Town. At present she is a teacher of English at Garlandale High School. She lives in a semi-communal house in Crawford with family, friends, two dogs and a cat, and is trying hard to create a garden, choreograph a dance, write poetry and attend COSAW meetings.

PHEDI TLHOBOLO is a poet, free thinker, translator, performer and musician. He was born on the 30th January 1967 in Lady Selbourne, Pretoria. He is a product of Seamoge Middle School and Ntolo High School. He appeared in numerous stage plays and was a lead vocalist for his band, Kwela Poets. His first professional stage appearance was in the play, *The Talking Ghosts* as a singer-actor-percussionist.

He groomed his artistic abilities by converting his

bedroom into a studio and a backyard university. His involvement in the South African Cultural politics has given birth to his uncompromising provocative views and his poetic style. He lives with his parents in Atteridgeville, Pretoria. He is at work on his first volume of poetry and a book of fairy tales for children. He writes and performs fulltime.

JAMES TWALA was born on the 29th of March 1941, in Natal. He started his schooling at Newclare Community School and developed an early interest in poetry. He started writing poems at high school just for fun. A number of his poems have appeared in various magazines, including an anthology comprised of the best poets in Africa and in *Ten Years of Staffrider*. He is married and lives in Soweto.